# Master Student Course Manual

*Faculty Advisors*

**Dean Mancina,**
**Golden West College, CA**

**Eldon L. McMurray**
**Utah Valley State College**

**Karl Mooney**
**University of Central Florida**

**Houghton Mifflin Company**

**Boston · New York**

Publisher: Patricia A. Coryell
Senior Sponsoring Editor: Mary Finch
Development Editor: Shani B. Fisher
Editorial Associate: Andrew M. Sylvester
Marketing Manager: Elinor Gregory
Marketing Assistant: Evelyn Yang
Manufacturing Manager: Karen Banks

College Survival
A Program of Houghton Mifflin Company
2075 Foxfield Drive, Suite 100
St. Charles, IL, 60174
1-800-528-8323
collegesurvival@hmco.com

Printed in the USA.

ISBN: 0-618-49329-8

1 2 3 4 5 6 7 8 9 – VHO – 09 08 07 06 05

# TABLE OF CONTENTS

## A letter to instructors from Faculty Advisor Dean Mancina

Dear Instructor,

**If you are a first time facilitator** of a course using a Master Student textbook, this Course Manual will assist you as part of an integrated package of instructor support materials that begins within these pages. Depending on the Master Student text you are using, you will also have an Annotated Instructor's Edition, an HM ClassPrep CD, and our dedicated Master Student Website.

**If you are a veteran user** of a Master Student textbook, you will remember the large 3-ring binder that served for many years as a reference tool for teachers in developing lesson plans, providing examples of course evaluation tools, and in-class activities that illustrated the articles in the text. This Course Manual, combined with the HM ClassPrep CD, and the resources available on the Master Student Website have now replaced that binder. With the available technologies, you have the capability of customizing content that has already been created to support the textbook you are using to be specific to your course. This material is easy to print, e-mail and share with your students, colleagues, or staff.

When I was a new instructor of the student success course at my college, I was overwhelmed. *Where do I begin*? My advice to you is that you start by browsing through the Course Manual, the HM ClassPrep CD, and the website. Here you will see more activities, ideas, and approaches than any one teacher could ever use in one class. The tools in this manual will help you whether your goal is to put together a new lesson plan in a pinch, or you want to revitalize one of your class sessions with a new guest speaker, activity, or assignment. Additionally, the articles in this manual may be an inspiration for you to create your own new activity or lecture. Consider sharing your creations with us by e-mailing them to collegesurvival@hmco.com. Your suggestion may appear in a future edition of the Course Manual or HM ClassPrep CD.

After I had developed the lesson plans for my course, and had been teaching the course for several semesters, a colleague told me of a wonderful activity she had just done with her students. She described it to me and I recalled reading it a long time ago in the Course Manual. My response was, "How did you get up the nerve to try that one! I took one look at it and thought it was too intense!" Then she showed me the exercise in the Course Manual, explained to me how she had followed it, and then shared the written Discovery Statements her students wrote after the exercise. I was sold! I tried the exercise the next semester, and it was a moving experience for my class.

My point is, by revisiting this Course Manual periodically you might discover an exercise or activity that, for whatever reason, you overlooked before. This manual is a guide to the other support materials, and ideas from hundreds of successful teachers who have used these tools in their classroom. This manual will help keep you and your course alive and fresh!

And, of course, anytime you feel stuck, you can always contact your College Survival Consultant at (800) 528-8323. They are familiar with the support materials and usually have more ideas up their sleeves. They are always happy to offer a suggestion or answer a question related to the teaching of your student success course.


Sincerely,

Dean Mancina
Faculty Advisor, *Becoming a Master Student*

**Master Student Map**
Eldon L. McMurray, Faculty Advisor, *Becoming a Master Student, Eleventh Edition*

One of the most exciting new features in the new *Master Student* textbooks is the Master Student Map (**M**etacognitive **A**pplication **P**rocess) located on the title page of each chapter. The Master Student Map is a reasoning model based on the Learning Style Inventory. Even the most inexperienced students can quickly begin to apply this simple, systematic process to monitor their thinking and learning. What makes this model so effective is that by utilizing the strengths of each learning style, students can implement the monitoring aspect of metacognition as soon as they achieve awareness.

Each category of the Master Student Map begins with a basic question designed to engage students' interest and lead to the important ideas presented in the chapter. A closer look at the design and formatting of each question in the Master Student Map will reveal the logic behind this innovative approach to introducing chapter topics.

*Why* **this chapter matters** …The role of this question is to encourage personal interest and a "need to know" in the learner. Initiating the Master Student Map with this type of question leads Mode 1 learners toward a deeper metacognitive understanding of their thinking, allowing them to call on principles within their prior knowledge that help structure the ideas in the chapter.

*What* **is included** … This question is followed by a list of specific, thought-provoking article titles from the chapter. This helps Mode 2 learners probe and analyze the factual and conceptual ideas presented in the chapter and become more aware of what will be expected of them.

*How* **you can use this chapter** … Mode 3 students will experience the impact of acclaimed features of *Becoming a Master Student,* such as the Discovery and Intention Journal Entry system, Power Processes, and Master Student Profiles, which uplift and inspire students to make personal commitments and set goals to accomplish. By consciously choosing their attitude about a chapter topic before they begin to study, students gain confidence in their own ability to initiate action and synthesize solutions to pressing problems. In this stage, have students go through the list of articles and mark the ones they predict they will know something about. The articles they do not mark indicate topics they are least familiar with. Having been made aware of knowledge gaps, they will have a better idea of what they need to study for tests.

**As you read, ask yourself** *What if* …Taking advantage of the action-oriented strength of Mode 4 learners, *What if?* questions lead to more lateral thinking and thus better-quality decisions. Specific skills do not necessarily transfer from one mental schema to another. Asking provocative *What if?* questions triggers the students' imagination to transfer skills and create new schema for developing skills in their other classes. Students are intrigued by inquiry rather than pat answers. *What if?* questions stimulate discussion and further the transfer of skills in situations outside the classroom as well.

Based on the latest theories of brain-active learning, the Master Student Map feature helps students activate relevant memories with regard to the subject matter in the chapter. Since all learning is dependent on prior knowledge, beginning each chapter with this reasoning model helps students in several ways. First, distractions can be reduced or eliminated, as the model allows students to study the most interesting or important topics first. Next, it helps increase the speed of students' learning by organizing the ideas in the beginning pages. Finally, it links all of the ideas in the entire textbook to the learning style of each student in a simple but powerful way.

Another important benefit of the Master Student Map is that it provides the instructor with a clear outline of what is going to be investigated in each chapter and a framework for guiding the discussion. Just by introducing the Master Student Map at the start of the chapter, instructors are using learning styles in their classroom. The four basic questions not only help instructors better understand what the students need to know but also serve as a catalyst for both pre- and post-assessment in the students' minds.

In a pilot study using this model, instructors at Utah Valley State College found these questions to be very helpful as teaching tools, primarily, because it gave them a place to begin instruction and a final destination.

Instructors who were more adept at viewing the curriculum in a holistic fashion were able to use this feature of overarching guiding questions to help them convey to students the big picture of the chapter in an efficient and a meaningful way. Those instructors who were more linear in their thinking leaned toward the *What* category of guiding questions and allowed their students to discover how the other questions fit in during the course of the discussion. This flexibility instilled confidence in the instructors to teach the magazine format of *Becoming a Master Student* in their own preferred style and enabled them to be more comfortable with the teaching process. Consequently, students reported high satisfaction with both the course instructor and the material.

Begin to use the Master Student Map now by reviewing the ancillary materials provided for you to accompany your textbook.

<u>**Course Manual**</u>
**WHY the Course Manual matters…**Being prepared and organized for teaching your course will help you to teach first year students the importance of becoming master students.
**WHAT is included…**The Course Manual includes information on how to write the course purpose statement, establish course objectives, determine instructional choices, integrate technology, assess assignments and exercises, identify evaluation criteria, and create and maintain a supportive classroom atmosphere for your students.
**HOW you can use this Course Manual…** Discover new ways to teach student success courses. Learn from instructors who have previously mastered teaching first year students.
**As you read, ask yourself WHAT IF…** I could use the materials in this course and apply it to the other disciplines I teach?

<u>**HM ClassPrep CD**</u>
**WHY the HM ClassPrep matters…**Having content electronically will allow you to customize content for your course.
**WHAT is included…**The HM ClassPrep CD includes chapter by chapter resources, PowerPoint slides, video lesson plans, and much more.
**HOW you can use this HM ClassPrep CD…** The HM ClassPrep CD is organized by asset and by chapter. If you want to see all of the PowerPoint slides you can select this by asset; if you prefer to review all of the resources available for Chapter Three, you can view the content by chapter.
**As you read, ask yourself WHAT IF…** I could enhance my course by adding campus specific information to the materials introduced in the maintext?

<u>**Master Student Web site**</u>
**WHY the Master Student website matters…**The Master Student Web site provides up-to-date information and resources to you and your students. Interactive exercises support concepts presented in the textbook to help you integrate technology into your course.

**WHAT is included...**The Master Student Web site has resources for both students and instructors. **HOW you can use this Web site...** Log onto http://masterstudent.hmco.com/ and view resources for students or instructors. Students will find additional exercises, articles and interactivity on the Web site. Instructors can access PowerPoint slides, information about events from College Survival, articles and other resources to support their teaching of their student success course. **As you read, ask yourself WHAT IF...** I could use the Web site to get students and faculty on my campus excited about using technology?

### Power Up! Four-in-One Power Process Video

**WHY the Power Up! Four-in-One Power Process Video matters...**Bringing a *guest speaker* to your course in the form of a video can help auditory and visual students learn new concepts. **WHAT is included...**The Power Up! video includes short segments on four of the Power Processes presented in the textbook: Ideas are tools, Notice your pictures, Find a bigger problem and Risk being a fool. **HOW you can use this video...** Enhance your students understanding of the Power Processes by showing them classroom and workplace applications as presented in this video. Use the before and after questions available on the HM ClassPrep CD. **As you read, ask yourself WHAT IF...** This video could help my students understand the Power Processes and how they can apply to their life in college and beyond?

### HM Assessment and Portfolio Builder

**WHY the HM Assessment and Portfolio Builder matters...**Beginning a conversation about goal setting, critical thinking and accomplishments in the first year of college is important to promoting positive career outcomes for students. **WHAT is included...** Students build a portfolio by responding to questions about their skills, attitudes, values and behaviors in four key life areas: Personal, Interpersonal, Career, and Community. The Accomplishments Report summarizes the results of their responses, and asks students to provide supporting evidence for questions where they rate themselves as highly proficient – great practice for critical thinking skills, as well as creating a résumé or preparing for interviews. The Accomplishments Report module also provides access to additional resources such as Houghton Mifflin's web-based Career Resource Center, which provides tips, exercises, articles and ideas to help students succeed on their journey from college to career. **HOW you can use this ancillary...** Package the HM Assessment and Portfolio Builder with your textbook and have students complete the assessment during the first few weeks of the course. Ask your students to revisit their assessment and Accomplishments Report throughout the semester and ask students to turn in an Accomplishments Report as part of a final assignment. **As you read, ask yourself WHAT IF...** This resource can help first year students be better prepared for selecting a major and going on an interview?

**Distinctions of *Becoming a Master Student***
Eldon L. McMurray, Faculty Advisor, *Becoming a Master Student, Eleventh Edition*

---

*Becoming a Master Student* is more than just a textbook. Students describe it as a life changing experience. The easy to read magazine article style entices students to read on through the purposeful, yet creatively arranged chapters. The interactive work text design has students write directly in the book so the density of the ideas is more evenly distributed. *Becoming a Master Student* completely addresses the three prime objectives of any first-year experience textbook, which are to assist students in developing the self-awareness, task awareness, and college awareness they need for college success in the new century.

Competing textbook publishers criticize *Becoming a Master Student*, suggesting there is no continuity and no prescriptive method given in the book. Nothing could be further from the truth. From the first chapter of this powerful text student learning is guided by personal assessments with built-in features like the Discovery Wheel and Learning Styles Inventory. This makes *Becoming a Master Student* the most comprehensively <u>assessment driven</u> student success text published today. When the student recognizes for him/herself what they need it is a more effective learning approach than giving a simple prescription like SQ3R. These carefully developed self-assessments strategically tie the chapters together in the priority order of what students will need most coming first by using dynamic features and activities designed to motivate them to be involved in the book and keep them involved.

Many of these trusted features have been in prior editions for twenty years and are effectively orchestrated to help students weave this "becoming" process into the fabric of their lives through the simple yet powerful Discovery and Intention Journal entry system. Each chapter is carefully aligned to accomplish the ultimate objective of self-mastery. Instructor's are fully supported by additional resources available in this Course Manual, in the Annotated Instructor's Edition, on the HM ClassPrep CD or on the website. They include a number of exercises, unifying themes, and a variety of activities that benefit students by helping them develop a level of mastery unrivaled by other first year experience textbooks. The exceptional school to career feature in *Becoming a Master Student,* called *Put it to Work*, or the new text, *From Master Student to Master Employee,* helps students to immediately identify the career application of the material they are learning in college This helps students to connect the skills they are learning with what they will apply in the world of work.

The following highlights the trusted features of *Master Student* and uses the Master Student Map to outline the benefits of the specific features to you as an instructor and to your students.

| Trusted Feature | Benefits of this Feature | | | |
|---|---|---|---|---|
| | **WHY?** | **WHAT?** | **HOW?** | WHAT IF? |
| **Discovery Wheel** | The Discovery Wheel is an important *first step* to a student success course because it functions as a means for the students to pre-assess their strengths and weakness and generates interest in the cohesive design of the textbook. | The Discovery Wheel is not a test. Students are encouraged to be honest and forthright as they respond to the statements about their experiences and practices such that results reflect an accurate picture of their current level of self-awareness. | As students score and total for each of the categories that relate to the chapters in the textbook, they graph their academic self-awareness on their Discovery Wheel. At the end of the book, they complete a second wheel as a post-course assessment. | The Discovery Wheel not only provides a valuable pre-assessment, it helps students get an idea of how *Becoming a Master Student* can help them immediately in their other classes and in their lives. |

| Trusted Feature | Benefits of this Feature | | | |
|---|---|---|---|---|
| | **WHY?** | **WHAT?** | **HOW?** | WHAT IF? |
| **Learning Styles Inventory (LSI)** | According to David Kolb's research, students generally perceive and process information in one of four ways, including feeling, watching, thinking, and doing. The four learning styles identified in this text help students to understand their personal preferences for learning. Through exercises and examples students learn to use their less dominant preferences to excel in the classroom and beyond. | The LSI is what makes the self-awareness component of *Becoming a Master Student* the so powerful. Through the cycle of learning, students will use a metacognitve application process to think critically and excel at decision making. | Significant learning experiences most often happen within a student's preferred learning style. Once students have identified a preference, they can learn how this awareness, the text will help them to employ all four styles by improving their use of the approaches that they often underutilize based on their preferences. | If the student is taught to process their learning experience using the aspects of critical thinking, by answering the related questions (why, what, how and what if), they will be empowered to make better decisions and become more balanced learners. |
| Trusted Feature | Benefits of this Feature | | | |
| | **WHY?** | **WHAT?** | **HOW?** | WHAT IF? |
| **Discovery and Intention Journal Entry System** | Discovery and Intention Statements allow students to achieve the necessary level of self-awareness to make the lasting changes they need to become a master student. | Each Journal Entry in the text is labeled as either Discovery Statements or Intention Statements. The Journal Entry contains a short set of suggestions that ask students to write about their discoveries, and based on these discoveries and the readings, their intentions. | Strategically spread throughout the text, students process discoveries into goals by writing down their intentions. The Journal Entries also ask students to analyze their discoveries to find potential solutions to their problems. | Discovery Statements are designed to help students achieve relevant discoveries about themselves as a learner. Through their intentions, they will predict answers to "What if?" questions. |
| Trusted Feature | Benefits of this Feature | | | |
| | **WHY?** | **WHAT?** | **HOW?** | WHAT IF? |
| **Variety of Critical Thinking Exercises** | Developing skills as a critical thinker is an important goal for first year students. | Significant concepts throughout the text are supported by exercises that take students through a process to make them more mindful thinkers. | Students complete a short exercise in each chapter related to critical thinking and the chapter topic. | Developing a more open-minded approach to thinking will help students develop the skills necessary to think critically across the disciplines. |

| Trusted Feature | Benefits of this Feature | | | |
|---|---|---|---|---|
| | **WHY?** | **WHAT?** | **HOW?** | WHAT IF? |
| **Power Processes** | Power Processes help students to achieve the level of consciousness needed to succeed in college. | In each chapter the most important mindset related to the study skill or life skill is set in an article called a Power Process. | Students read and or dramatize these concepts and work towards the connections between their school responsibilities and the world around them. | Understanding the bigger picture and gaining the necessary mindset for success will help students complete their goals in college and beyond. |

| Trusted Feature | Benefits of this Feature | | | |
|---|---|---|---|---|
| | **WHY?** | **WHAT?** | **HOW?** | WHAT IF? |
| **Master Student Profiles** | For some students having a role model helps them more than anything else. The Master Student Profiles help students to see the importance of their efforts on success. | Each chapter has a Master Student selected because of their connection to the chapter topic and Power Process article. | Students will read the profile and make their own connections between the profile and the chapter. | If students apply the master student qualities they identify as important to the featured Master Student in the profile, they can work towards incorporating these traits into their persona. |

| Trusted Feature | Benefits of this Feature | | | |
|---|---|---|---|---|
| | **WHY?** | **WHAT?** | **HOW?** | WHAT IF? |
| **Student Voices** | Quotations from students and workplace professionals highlight firsthand master student success stories.. | This feature allows students to make connections with other master students just like themselves by gaining new insights as they work through this textbook. | Reading these brief statements helps students see how the tactics and insights that they have gained compare to previous student's journey through the text. | What if one of the insights your students achieved could help another student as they word towards mastery? This sharing is empowering. |

| New Feature | Benefits of this Feature | | | |
|---|---|---|---|---|
| | **WHY?** | **WHAT?** | **HOW?** | WHAT IF? |
| **Master Student Map** | Metacognition involves asking the question "why?" when considering various topics, activities, or assignments. The answer leads to a realization or understanding of the importance of the effort. | The question associated with analysis is "what?" Answering this question helps students identify essential elements of course content and the resources this new knowledge provides. | Synthesis requires that an instructor answer "how?" This aspect involves aligning the parts identified during the analysis stage into a meaningful sequence | Finally, application raises the question "what if?" This stage involves creative application in the classroom to bring the curriculum into student's reality. It allows them to transfer student succcss strategies into all aspects of education and life. |

| New Feature | Benefits of this Feature | | | |
|---|---|---|---|---|
| | **WHY?** | **WHAT?** | **HOW?** | **WHAT IF?** |
| **Improved Introduction with new Power Process** | Developing a passion for the value of education requires students get an idea of what they want. | A new Power Process, Discover what you want, expands on the ideas presented in the "What do You Want" video. The comprehensive introduction sets the stage for this course. | Students create a view of what they want from their education and begin to set goals for themselves right from the outset. | Students may understand what they want, but not what they need. This leads them right into the Discovery Wheel (in Chapter 1) where they can identify these needs. |

| New Feature | Benefits of this Feature | | | |
|---|---|---|---|---|
| | **WHY?** | **WHAT?** | **HOW?** | **WHAT IF?** |
| **New Learning Styles Application (LSA)** | It is vital for the learner to be aware of their learning style preference. It provides a frame of reference of where significant learning experiences occur most often—within a learner's preferred style | At the end of each chapter, the LSA guides students through the process of using each of the learning styles to develop a comprehensive understanding of the chapter contents. | If students are taught to process their learning experiences by answering questions related to four key aspects of critical thinking and to each learning style, they will be empowered with the strengths of each style to learn. | There is limited utility to knowing about learning styles unless students work towards utilizing different styles by completing the LSA. Students will learn to avoid repeating their mistakes, consciously know exactly why they succeeded, identify what they need to know, and understand how to repeat their successes to make better quality decisions in any learning situation. |

| New Feature | Benefits of this Feature | | | |
|---|---|---|---|---|
| | **WHY?** | **WHAT?** | **HOW?** | **WHAT IF?** |
| **Put it to Work** | The skills and attitudes students can develop from reading *Becoming a Master Student* translate into the skills and attitudes needed to be successful in today's dynamic workplace. | Transferable skills are highlighted in this feature bringing into focus the workplace applications of key concepts covered in each chapter. | Reading these selections will shift the mindset of students into those of employees. This helps students to be more goal-oriented as they conclude each chapter. | If students understand the ways that these skills transfer to the workplace, they may be more willing to put the effort required into making the skill and attitude stick. |

| New Feature | Benefits of this Feature | | | |
|---|---|---|---|---|
| | **WHY?** | **WHAT?** | **HOW?** | WHAT IF? |
| **Technology Chapter** | Information technology pervades our lives. Computers are found on our desktops, in our libraries, and on our laps. Students need to develop a level of knowledge and competency with computers if they are to succeed in college and beyond. | Courses in higher education are no longer divided into separate categories—distance learning (delivered exclusively over the Internet) versus traditional courses (delivered by human beings standing in front of a classroom). | Students will learn to become effective on-line learners. They will learn to find useful, accurate information on the Internet and gain a basic understanding of how technology and college life are integrated. | A new model has emerged: the hybrid course. Hybrid courses combine online instruction with class meetings and textbooks. What if students applied their study skills to an online environment? And what if they do not? |

| New Feature | Benefits of this Feature | | | |
|---|---|---|---|---|
| | **WHY?** | **WHAT?** | **HOW?** | WHAT IF? |
| **Earlier placement of money management** | The ability to manage economic resources is vital to successfully navigating the college experience. | Moving this important section closer to the beginning of the book will help students address their financial planning needs at the start of the semester. | The students will read the article, analyze their money needs and learn strategies to create a workable budget. | Many students have never had to live within a budget or have limited experience managing their own money and credit cards wisely. |

| New Feature | Benefits of this Feature | | | |
|---|---|---|---|---|
| | **WHY?** | **WHAT?** | **HOW?** | WHAT IF? |
| **New Master Student Profiles** | These profiles highlight examples of master student qualities and bring the Power Process articles to life. | One Master Student is highlighted per chapter. New Master Students are featured along with a new Master Student Hall of Fame on the website. | The characteristics of a Master Student are listed in an article in Chapter One. Article content relates to these qualities as well as the Power Process article. | A Master Student Hall of Fame provides additional information for inspiration on the Master Student Website that includes biographical information and links for getting started on further research. |

# Developing Your Student Success Course

## Essentials for planning and instruction

College Survival, Freshman Seminar, University 101, and the First-Year Experience are among the various names for the most researched and results-oriented course in higher education. This course is designed for learners in their first term or year at a university or college. According to Aubrey Forrest's report for the National Center for Advancement of Educational Practices entitled Increasing Student Competence and Persistence:

> *Probably the single most important move an institution can make to increase student persistence to graduation is to ensure that students receive the guidance they need at the beginning of the journey through college to graduation. At its best, this guidance system should include the following feature: New student orientation should continue as a formal course during their first term on campus.*

The purpose of a student success course is to assist students in navigating the terrain of higher education, to improve their academic performance, to help them determine their strengths and goals, and to encourage them to implement strategies to enhance their personal, academic, and career success.

The content of a student success course will be influenced by the institutional mission statement, the instructor, the outcomes expected by the administration, and the students in the course.

The content of a student success course might include the following:
- The history of higher education
- Academic proficiency skills
- Self-assessment and inventory
- Critical thinking and writing
- Diversity and international relations
- Technology and online learning skills
- Listening and speaking skills
- Modes of inquiry
- Oral presentation skills
- Service learning
- Information literacy and library skills
- Collaborative learning activities
- Effective use of learning resources and tutors
- Campus and community support services
- Research skills, documentation, and academic writing
- Career planning and development of transferable skills
- Civility in the classroom
- Academic integrity

Competency objectives for a student success course might include the following:
- To assess and inventory current strengths and areas for growth
- To increase awareness of beliefs, choices, and behaviors
- To provide use of, knowledge of, and access to campus support staff and programs
- To explore and enhance transferable academic, personal, and career skills

2

Expectations of student classroom behavior might include exhibiting the following qualities of exceptional employees:
- Self-knowledge and insight
- Preparedness and punctuality
- Involvement and initiative
- Attentive listening skills
- Critical reflection and writing skills
- Creative problem-solving skills
- Respect for the opinions and values of others
- Curiosity and a desire for lifelong learning
- Positive contributions to the climate of the workplace
- Thorough, timely, and thoughtful completion of tasks
- Active participation
- Application of strategies in other areas of study and life

Elements of assessment in a student success course might include the following:
- Reading assignments
- Written exercises, Journal Entries, and classroom activities
- Individual and small group presentations
- Quizzes
- Conversation and discussion
- Projects
- Final examination
- Evaluation
- Portfolio development

An effective course framework might be described as follows:
- Credit-bearing
- Built into the curriculum as a core requirement
- Presented over the first term
- Involving 30 or more contact hours
- Taught by the best instructors
- Well scheduled
- Clearly valuable to students and staff

Outcomes of a student success course might include the following:
- Enhanced student performance
- Increased grade point average (GPA)
- Greater number of courses attempted and completed
- Persistence to graduation
- Enhanced faculty satisfaction
- Partnership in the learning environment

## First steps

Congratulations! You are teaching a student success course!

Consider this book the "owner's manual" for creating your course. This manual is designed to streamline your efforts and to give you the best suggestions collected from more than 10,000 educators and the consultants of College Survival, who have more than 20 years of experience implementing premier student success courses.

You might not choose to explore every section. You might start with the topics about which you require the most guidance or anticipate struggle. You might feel very confident and still choose to enhance or revitalize your areas of expertise.

This is a guide for designing your course and exploring major subjects relevant to all student success courses. This guide is created for instructor's using (or planning to use) *Becoming a Master Student, From Master Student to Master Employee*, and *Becoming a Master Student Athlete*. Your HM ClassPrep CD-ROM offers you chapter-by-chapter resources and is specific to the title you are using. If you do not have an HM ClassPrep CD for your text, contact your local sales representative or your College Survival consultant. Your planning will result in the creation of a course that will reflect the uniqueness of your teaching style, the personality of your students, and the culture of your campus. Consider this manual as a springboard to many possibilities. Adopt and modify these ideas for your course purpose and structure, and for the outcomes you plan to achieve.

If you have limited time for planning, please do three things:

1. Do the first 15-minute exercise the student edition of the book, labeled Textbook Reconnaissance. Touch every page of the text. This will give you an overview and will spark your imagination about what to highlight for students.

2. Apply the sample principles of this exercise to the *Course Manual* to familiarize yourself with the topics. Make note of the most relevant information to you as you begin planning your course. Consider re-doing this exercise anytime you feel you need new ideas.

3. As part of the Master Student family, you are now partners in success with Houghton Mifflin Student Success Programs and College Survival. As a member of the network of professionals using a *Master Student* product, we can assist you in a number of ways— through support in setting up your course, in training your faculty and in energizing you at our conferences. Just as a teacher will provide information and support to students and will help them choose effective personal and professional strategies, the consultants of College Survival will provide you with information and support for the creative process of designing a course for your students.

### Student Success versus Study Skills Courses
Dean Mancina, Faculty Advisor, *Becoming a Master Student, Eleventh Edition*

Many years ago, I coordinated the peer Tutoring Program on my campus. Students came into the center with academic difficulties in one or more courses. The tutors helped them, and they did better in their classes. The next semester, they often returned, and we repeated the cycle. Tutors reported to me that in most cases the student's problem was not the subject matter, but a lack of effective student

4

skills. This was curious to me, since my campus offered a study skills course, but even though we had more than 10,000 students, the course rarely filled. And, we only offered one section each year!

As a result of my research, I discovered College Survival and *Becoming A Master Student*. I returned to my campus and spent two years developing and seeking approval for a Student Success course. Our Study Skills course was a credit/no credit only course that ran one half of a semester, and was non-transferable. Offered by our English department, the course was buried amongst the diverse course offerings in that department.

As a result of my consultations with College Survival, and after surveying the needs of the students on our campus, the following features were important parts of the course I proposed and was successful in getting approved:

- Letter graded course (with credit/no credit as an option)
- 3.0 units (a full-semester length course)
- Transferable credit

These were factors that students told me were important when they made their decisions about which courses to take.

We started with two sections, and have grown now to an average of 38 sections per year. Unlike many colleges, our course is not required. If it were required, we would have four times the number of sections!

As you begin to define and develop the goals for your course, it is important to note some of the distinctions between "study skills" and "student success" courses. Student Success courses take a holistic approach in helping students perform better in college. Both types of courses teach, for example, note taking, test taking, and memory skills, but student success courses also include topics such as planning, thinking, communicating, health, and technology. Studies have shown this approach to be effective in helping students get better grades, complete more units, and reduce the chance that they will drop out of college.

Get started developing your student success course by understanding the major themes of the Master Student textbooks.

## Values-Based Education: Understanding the themes of *Master Student*

*Master Student* is unique because it is based on a particular value system that is incorporated in all of the study skills throughout the book. This system includes the following five values:
1. Focused attention
2. Personal responsibility
3. Integrity
4. Risk taking
5. Contribution

These values are discussed in a general way in several of the Power Processes presented throughout *Master Student* and are the foundation of each of the study skills, life skills, and activities presented in the text. For example, when presenting the study skill of note taking, the text is really introducing the concepts of focusing attention, contributing to fellow students by sharing notes, and taking risks by using notes as an opportunity to ask questions of teachers. Also, when talking about time management, the text frequently presents the ideas of focusing attention, being responsible for one's use of time, and practicing integrity.

These values show up even more obviously in the life skills that the text describes as communication, leadership, stress management, and so on. Throughout the course, as an instructor you can build on these values and reinforce the fundamental concepts of the text by referring back to the Power Processes. Or consider posting the five values and asking students to find examples of the application of these values as they are used throughout the book, presented in class lectures or mentioned by guest speakers.

## Student Success course philosophy

The underlying philosophy of student success courses is based on the following three assumptions:

1. There are no secrets.
2. There are no victims.
3. There are no solos.

**There are no secrets.** It is usually a mistake to assume that students come to school prepared. As they begin college, they face major changes in their environments and lifestyles. Assuming that they know how to study and how to be effective students is often inaccurate. The fact that students have been in school for years is no guarantee that they have mastered the process of learning.

Most students enroll in college with both the ability and the motivation to succeed. During exit interviews many educators discover that what students lacked was a clear understanding of specific strategies to get what they wanted from school. Most dropout statistics can be lowered when students become aware of learning strategies, experiment with them, find those that work, and turn them into habits that they adopt as part of their daily routines. *Master Student* and the course outlined in this course manual present clear, positive, appealing images of behaviors that lead to success. As students begin to experiment with and adopt these behaviors, they are on their way to achieving their goals. The Power Process "Discover what you want" in the introduction of the text begins to guide students through the goal setting process, more specifically covered in Chapter 2, Planning.

**There are no victims.** Blaming other people or circumstances does not empower us to get what we want. Even blaming ourselves gets in the way of success. Blaming cheats us of the experience of taking full responsibility for our lives. Taking responsibility opens the door to making choices that allow us to be in control. The Power Process "I create it all" in the text presents this idea.

**There are no solos.** Human beings are social creatures. Other people play a powerful role in the development of our own values, belief systems, and behaviors. A supportive environment is a critical element of student success. The Student Success course provides an opportunity for students to connect with others and form mutually beneficial relationships. Students can also become aware of the many resources and programs that can promote their success. These ideas are developed throughout the text, with an emphasis on resources in the Introduction, and relationship building in the Communicating chapter.

Students at each school and the purpose and focus of the course at each institution will be different. *Master Student* was designed to give students a variety of topics and ideas. This manual was created to assist you in selecting material most appropriate for your students and course purpose and in fulfilling your institutional mission statement of how your graduates will be unique.

6

The first question to ask yourself when planning is: Who will take the course? Many colleges across the country require that their new students participate in a Student Success course. They feel that this course will be an educational foundation for students in their day-to-day college courses and as they link their knowledge to their future careers. The skills undergraduates use to be effective students (time management, critical thinking, writing, communication skills, etc.) are the same skills that will assist them in becoming effective employees. Significant research over the past 25 years acknowledges the value that participating in a life and study skills course has for all new students. Many schools require that certain populations take this course. Some offer it only to honors students or to those students who are accepted provisionally or have low scores on entrance exams, SATs, or ACTs. Some require all developmental students to take this course. Be clear about who will be in your classes; this knowledge will assist you in writing a clear purpose statement and in stating the objectives for your course.

Whether you have heterogeneous or homogeneous groups, be sensitive to the needs and concerns of your students and consider how to involve them effectively in your classes.

## Adapting to the culture of higher education

Even though the average age of students is older than it once was, many students still go directly from high school to college. They enter higher education with no idea of the changes in expectations from high school classrooms to the college environment. As you think about creating the future of Student Success courses, consider the following student populations that you list below. Consider the special support services these students will require as well as the diverse gifts they will bring to your college community.

What are the changing demographics and students' issues represented at your college?

_____
_____
_____

## Authoring your course purpose statement

A written purpose is the foundation of your course and the yardstick you can use to measure its effectiveness. Recopying or rewriting the Student Success course purpose statement in your own words can provide you with greater confidence and clarity of intention. Consider the following questions when authoring your course's purpose statement:

1.      What is your college's mission statement? How will this course promote the attitudes, behaviors, and choices your graduates are expected to exhibit in the world?

_____
_____
_____
_____

2.      What is the profile of the students your college or university serves? What distresses and delights you about your students? What are the very best qualities of your graduates?

_____
_____
_____
_____

3.  What do your upper class students say they learned "the hard way" or wish they could have done differently as first-year students?

    _____
    _____
    _____
    _____

4.  What do the first-year core curriculum faculty members say are the challenges that hamper first-year student success in their academic discipline? How could this course prepare students for the differences between their secondary school experiences and the expectations of higher education?

    _____
    _____
    _____
    _____
    _____

5.  What would you say to first-year students if you had one last lecture to give?

    _____
    _____
    _____
    _____

6.  How would you sequence the Student Success course topics and experiences if the students were in your class only for the first six weeks of the term? (Note: The first six weeks are considered the most crucial period for new students, according to retention research. By the sixth week, if students do not experience a sense of belonging and find value in their courses, they often decide that they want to leave, even if they actually endure for the rest of the term.)

    _____
    _____
    _____
    _____

## Sample purpose statements

It is interesting how authoring a purpose statement reflects the values of the writer. The following are sample purpose statements that educators have written during this exercise at College Survival workshops or trainings.

**The purpose of this professional seminar is** to empower students to achieve peak performance at an academic, a personal, and a professional level through the use of proven educational and mental strategies.

**The purpose of this course is** to give students an opportunity to create and change their habits and vision to allow themselves to have a rich, full, and rewarding personal, scholastic, and professional life through the adoption of positive strategies and techniques.

**The purpose of the freshman seminar is** to create an environment for honors students that enables them to grow personally, academically, and professionally. Therefore, the course will stress growth and personal and interpersonal development and provide specific information about the college and higher education in general.

8

**The purpose of the orientation course is** to assist the undecided student in improving academic skills, choosing a career, and enjoying the college experience.

**The mission of College Foundations is** to help students develop the skills essential to becoming the best they can be in all areas of life.

**To provide** life skills for cadets/students to enable them to be successful (by their definition) in both college and their future careers, military or civilian.

**The purpose of this course is** to provide students with an opportunity to cultivate the skills, values, and attitudes necessary to become confident, capable students and contributing community members (or to enrich them academically, personally, and professionally).

**The purpose of Student Learning Strategies is** to create experiences for students that will assist them in developing values, skills, and techniques that will enrich them academically, professionally, and personally.

**The purpose of this College Success Skills class is** to provide the tools that enable and empower a person to become or improve as a student and to succeed in all areas of life as a caring, aware, and responsible human being.

**The purpose of EDU 102 is** to create an opportunity to expose students to academic and personal tools that will help them to enhance their strengths, to acknowledge and develop their weaknesses, and to learn to adopt the tools in such a way that they can be modified for lifelong learning (enhancement).

**The purpose of this College Success Skills course is** to provide students an opportunity to adopt techniques and strategies to enhance their success in school and in their jobs and their ability to contribute to the lives of others.

**The purpose of BUS 105 is** to facilitate and promote student success—both academic and career successes. It is to serve as a "fertile ground" on which students have the opportunity to begin to sow the seeds of success by developing themselves personally, academically, and professionally.

**Our mission is** to empower and inspire students to be successful, by their standards, in their lives (personal and professional) and in their studies by learning strategies (styles, changing of habits, and so on) that they can immediately and continuously apply throughout life and that enable them to leave the course with confidence, enthusiasm, and a passion to succeed.

**The purpose of SLS 1101 is** to provide an opportunity to develop skills and manners that will lead to success academically and in other areas of life; in short, to become and remain a student.

## Refining Your Course Purpose

One purpose for a Student Success course is to provide an opportunity for students to learn and to adopt methods to promote their achievements in school. Every lecture, exercise, guest speaker, conversation/sharing, or other activity done in class has this purpose. Reminding students of their own purpose for being in school helps them stay focused. Purpose gives meaning and importance to daily routines. The intention of a Student Success course is made clear by closely examining its purpose. You can review the course's purpose with students by discussing each of the following key phrases.

**Purpose**—Everyone has untapped potential. *Becoming a Master Student* is a lifelong process. The purpose does not prescribe a final destination. Rather, it suggests a direction of growth and learning. It is impossible, for example, to arrive at a destination called "East." Traveling east makes more sense than reaching a goal called "East." Ask your students to explain why. We can use a purpose as we would use a direction on a compass—to continually monitor our progress.

**Provide an opportunity**—*The American Heritage Dictionary* defines the word *teach* as "to cause to learn." A cause is defined as a person or thing "responsible for an action or a result." Since each student is responsible for her own learning, no one else can be the source or cause of that learning, so we have an interesting dilemma. No one can cause another person's learning, and teaching is defined as causing another's learning. There is only one possible conclusion: Teaching is impossible. Don't be discouraged. Teaching as a profession is not in jeopardy. Even though teaching in this sense is impossible, teachers nevertheless have a challenging and useful job. They provide an opportunity for students to learn. They invite students to learn. Teachers can set the stage in the most effective way possible for learning to take place. They can also convey that the responsibility for learning rests with the students.

Learning, defined as "the act . . . of gaining knowledge or skill," is not only possible, it is the most natural act humans can perform. It begins before birth and continues throughout life. Teachers are responsible for providing an opportunity. Students are responsible for learning.

**Learn and adopt**—Knowing what is needed to be successful, however, is not enough. Students might know many of the strategies suggested and not use them. They might know which behaviors would promote their success and not adopt them. Unless strategies for success are put into action, they are useless. This course encourages students to learn and to adopt methods that will enable them to be successful in school. This activity often requires behavioral change. Selling students on the idea of changing their behavior is the ultimate challenge of this course. Shifts in attitudes, values, and beliefs accompany shifts in behavior.

**Methods**—Most of the course involves concrete techniques and specific strategies for success. Even the parts that are more philosophical in nature can be used as tools to generate a successful experience at school and beyond. See *Becoming a Master Student* for a discussion of the Power Process "Ideas are tools."

**Successful in school**—No one description of success is appropriate for everyone. People are different and so are their pictures of success. This course is not intended to promote success as defined by parents, teachers, or administrators. Each unique student defines success individually.

Being a successful student might expand easily and naturally into learning more general life skills and ensuring success later in life and in one's lifework.

## Possible Course Titles

Academic Development Seminar
Academic Resources
Achieving Academic Success
Becoming a Lifelong Learner
Becoming a Master Student
Beyond Creativity
Career Development
College Learning Techniques
College Preparation
College Skills
College Success Skills
College Survival
College Survival Seminar
College Survival Skills
College Survival: Soaring with the Eagles
College Survival Training
Communications
Developing Study Skills
Discovery and Experience Through Liberal Arts
Educational and Life Planning
Efficient Personal Study Skills
Freshman Foundations
Freshman Orientation
Freshman Seminar
Human Development
Human Potential
Interpersonal Relations
Introduction to College Study
Introduction to University Studies
Invitation to Success

Issues in College Life
Keys to Success
Learning Techniques
Life Enhancement
Life Learning Skills
Life Management Skills and College
Master Student
Mastering Skills for College Survival
Mastery Skills
New Student Seminar
Personal Awareness
Personal Study Efficiency
Planning for Academic Success
Practical Approaches to Efficient Study
Preparation Skills for College Success
Principles of Academic and Personal Development
Professional Development
Psychology of College Survival
Resources Development
Self-assessment Career Development
Strategies for Academic Excellence
Strategies for Success: Freshman Seminar
Student Mentor Program
Study Techniques
Surviving and Thriving in College
Take Charge of Your Learning
Transitions
University Experience
University 101
University Survival and Study Skills

# Planning your Student Success course

This section can help you select topics to best fulfill your course purpose and to address the issues facing first-year students at your college. Many schools customize Student Success courses to address one, two, or all three of the major themes in the *Master Student* text you are using:

1. **First Steps**—encourage students to examine their current skills and assess areas for potential growth. Such scrutiny offers students the chance for reflection, self-knowledge, and development. Students begin to discover what they want, and work towards achieving these goals.

2. **Academic skills** (time, memory, reading, notes, and tests)—provide students with the knowledge and opportunity to improve scholastic skills and use techniques necessary for success in their core curriculum courses.

3. **Life and workplace skills** (thinking, communicating, diversity, technology, and health)—present students with opportunities to practice healthy lifestyles, utilize technology resources, embrace diversity, improve communication to enrich relationships, and prepare for their careers by identifying transferable skills.

Teachers of different courses might establish a module, workshop, or seminar approach for teaching these areas in one semester or two semesters. While these are the primary themes of a Student Success course, you will find that critical thinking, personal responsibility, integrity, and expanding the role of the scholar will also be incorporated into each of these areas. Your individual college or university will emphasize the goals of its mission statement and showcase the people and programs available to support its students during their transition to college life.

This section of the Course Manual provides an overview of the topics that you can include under the three themes of *Master Student* and offers models to promote partnership in the learning process, methods of instruction, and enhancement activities. Most teachers and students benefit by having a clear sense of where they are going. This section will help you express the purpose and benefits of each of these three themes in your own words to engage your students' interest in establishing goals and achieving academic, personal, and career success.

## Maximizing the effectiveness of your Student Success course

In developing or revising your course, please consider including all of the following elements, which have shown to maximize the course effectiveness.

- The course is offered for credit.

- Students spend at least 30 contact hours in class.

- The course is taught over time (spread out over an entire term rather than during one or two weeks).

- Teachers are notified at least one month in advance that they will be teaching the course.

- Teachers are personally interested in teaching this course.

12

- Retention data on entering first-term students is maintained.

- Weekly quizzes and evaluations are given.

- End-of-term course and teacher evaluations are completed.

- Course materials (the Annotated Instructor's Edition (if available) the Course Manual, the HMClassPrep CD-ROM, URL for web site exercises (masterstudent.college.hmco.com), videotapes, and the telephone number for support services (800-528-8323)) are given to teachers at least one month before the beginning of the course.

- Teachers are aware of and use the toll-free telephone consultation services available from College Survival.

- Teachers schedule at least one hour of preparation time for each hour of class time.

- Teachers are trusted by students and have good rapport with them.

- Student performance is evaluated (on either a pass/fail or graded basis).

- A seven-part format is followed (that is, the course is taught with a balance among lectures, exercises, guest speakers and videotapes, conversations and sharing, quizzes and evaluations, previews and reviews, and assignments).

- Teachers assigned to teach the course are trusted and respected by the administration and other faculty.

## Benefits for the entire campus community

Effective Student Success courses benefit everyone at an educational institution. Students define their goals with clarity and gather the tools that can help them to achieve their dreams. Obviously, students win when they experience success. Educators experience the delight of daring to encourage students' dreams. They are in the ideal position to contribute significantly to the quality of students' lives as well as to their students' academic success. Many educators say that teaching this course demanded their best, but it was well worth the effort and actually reminded them of why they became teachers.

Administrators are also committed to students success but often do not get a chance to witness the tangible results that confirm hat what they are doing works. Sharing the course evaluations and research helps them to realize that this course does impact retention of first-year students. Administrators win when they can direct a program that is getting results.

Additionally, the entire staff of the campus wins when students are satisfied by their experience and speak well of the institution. They can take pride in working on a campus that effectively serves students. Admissions staff benefits from the persona referrals of satisfied students who become alums and generous donors because of memories of exceptional care and concern. Also, parents and other family members consider the institution worthy of their investments.

A Student Success course well planned and facilitated by a caring and competent teacher gives students a chance to make lifelong friends as well as to develop a love for learning. It can also assist students as they navigate a very exciting time in their first term of their first year at college.

## Getting to know your book

The format of the *Master Student* texts is different from other textbooks. The worktext is organized in self-contained, independent chapters and sections. The chronological sequence in which the material is presented can be changed to fit students needs and logistical circumstances. For example, review the Discovery Wheel in Chapter 1. Your students can help you to create your course syllabus by identifying areas in which they need to build more skills. This upfront assessment of strengths and weaknesses helps students to see the big picture of what your course is about, and where they can work towards improving their skills and confidence. More information on creating your course syllabus in this way is available on your HM Class Prep CD.

*Master Student* uses the same technique that advertisers employ: repetition. It works. A spiral approach to repetition takes hundreds of different ideas and weaves them into a unified whole. Ideas covered in later chapters appear briefly in earlier chapters. Ideas developed previously are reinforced later.

**Design** The student text was designed to appeal to students. Its physical size and bright color are not accidents. It is too big to fit easily in most drawers and too expensive-looking to throw away. Consequently, it will sit on a shelf and invade the student's space.

The book conveys the critically important message of taking self-responsibility. Ideas in the text are presented like a series of advertisements for various behaviors that promote student success. There are illustrations, photographs, and many short, self-contained messages. The magazine-style format, humor, and conversational tone are intended to make reading this book an enjoyable as well as valuable experience.

The worktext's pages are perforated so that they can be torn out and reinserted easily. This format makes selected pages more convenient for teachers to college. Teachers are encouraged to have their students hand in some of the exercises, quizzes, and Journal Entries. Students can then easily reinsert the pages by wedging them back into the spine. Pages reinserted in this manner will remain secure.

**Rationale** The techniques presented in the *Master Student* text are effective. No amount of expert testimony is as convincing as a student's own experience, so students are encouraged to try these methods. Practicality is the key. Students are not told why these techniques work. This is not a book about educational theory or psychology. It does not provide students with the means to psychoanalyze themselves. The purpose of the worktext is to list methods that can be used immediately to produce results.

Not all of the techniques in this book apply to all students in all situations. What works for one student may not work for another. What works for one student in one situation may not work for that same students when faced with a different task. This worktext does not moralize and make absolute predictions about student behavior. Students don't want to be lectured, and their experiences will probably differ from whatever is presenting in any book. Individualizing the material is a matter of trial and error. The spirit of the worktext is to encourage students to experiment with the ideas that are presented and to adopt those that work.

14

**Audience** Each of the *Master Student* textbooks is intended for first-term college students of all ages. Each of these texts is designed to meet the needs of a wide variety of traditional and nontraditional students as well as student from any ethnic, racial, and cultural backgrounds. *Master Student* textbooks include examples, role models, pertinent articles, and suggestions for students. The ability to communicate across cultures is important for all students. The ideas and techniques in the worktext are as applicable to four-year liberal arts programs as they are to short technical programs. In fact, learning how to learn, which is what *Master Student* is all about, is appropriate anywhere learning is taking place.

Our new titles, *From Master Student to Master Employee*, and *Becoming a Master Student Athlete* were created with the intention of providing specific strategies, examples and techniques to two specific audiences. *From Master Student to Master Employee* emphasizes career readiness, workplace application and transferable skills throughout the text, with new chapters on Career Planning and Mastering Work. The book helps students to understand the value of continuously expanding their knowledge and skills to remain competitive in today's job market. Students returning to school after time in the workplace will also begin to identify how the workplace skills they already have can be utilized in the classroom.

*Becoming a Master Student Athlete* is targeted towards first-year student athletes who are learning to balance their time in the classroom with their time practicing and playing their sport. Recent, more rigorous changes to academic requirements for student athletes make it essential to provide these students with the skills and strategies they need to succeed academically and maintain eligibility. *Becoming a Master Student Athlete* includes exercise and activities that have a hands-on approach that will be popular with kinesthetic learners. Articles, examples, Master Student Profiles and the art program are relevant and engaging for the student athlete. This text also helps student athletes prepare for life beyond college by addressing the importance of major exploration and career options.

*Becoming a Master Student,* Canadian Fourth Edition is specifically geared towards Canadian students. Revised coverage of money management, writing (including an update based on the latest Canadian Writer's Style Handbook) workplace skills, nutrition, and multiculturalism enhance this new edition to address the needs of the Canadian Student. In addition, new career-related information from the Conference Board of Canada's Employability Skills 2000+ has been incorporated to help students develop the skills most valued by employers

**Worktext content** Common elements in each chapter of the book will help your students to easily navigate the text. Begin with the **chapter opener page.** This page includes several key elements: the chapter title, an image representing the ideas presented in the chapter, inspirational quotations, and the new *Master Student Map.* This map is a tool that students can use to understand *why* the chapter is important, *what* is included in the chapter, *how* the materials in the chapter can be used, and begin to ask themselves as they read *what if* they could use these ideas in other areas of their life. The Master Student Map previews chapter content, connects to the Learning Style Inventory (in Chapter 1) and provides a metacognitive tool that starts each chapter off using a common critical thinking framework. The *Master Student Map* helps instructors to address the needs of all students in their course from the outset, no matter what their preference for learning (as identified in the Learning Styles Inventory).

The page to the right of the chapter opener page students will find an introduction to the chapter and the first **Journal Entry** of each chapter. Journal entries are insights generated by writing. By writing Discovery Statements and Intention Statements (outlined in the Introduction), students examine their experiences, evaluate their behavior, explore their values, determine what (if anything) they want to modify, and form specific action plans for achieving what they want to modify, and form specific action plans for achieving what they want.

**Exercises** invite student participation. Students can translate what they are learning into experiences that are personally relevant. This process encourages students to take responsibility for their own education. **Practicing Critical Thinking** exercises (or **Thinking Critically in the Classroom** and **Thinking Critically in the Workplace** in *From Master Student to Master Employee*) provides the opportunity to focus on skills such as summarizing, uncovering assumptions, detecting logical fallacies, and considering alternate points of view. These critical thinking exercises ask students to use a higher level of thinking that expands as they work through the topics in the textbook.

At the end of the chapter, students will find a new toolbar that highlights the features that regularly appear at the conclusion of each chapter. The **Power Process** is a unique motivational article that empowers success through the application of strategies that relate to a wide variety of circumstances, issues, and problems. A new feature, **Put it to work**, reinforces transferability of skills by encouraging students to think critically about how concepts and techniques they are learning in school might apply to workplace applications. (In *From Master Student to Master Employee*, **Put it to work** is replaced by a **Career application,** a case study that helps students take concepts form the book and apply it to a workplace scenario. These cases highlight transferable skills, connect with SCANS competencies, and illustrate for students how to make successful transitions from success in school to success on the job. Each career application case study is followed by four fill-in questions.) The **Quiz** allows students to assess their comprehension of the materials covered in each chapter. On the flip side of the quiz, students will find the **Learning Styles Application.** The Learning Styles Application is linked to the content of each chapter and prompts students to practice four distinct ways of processing and perceiving ideas as identified in the Learning Style Inventory. It also provides closure by asking students again to think about *why, what, how* and *what if* questions first identified in the Master Student Map. These two pages can easily be submitted for grading and then returned to the textbook. The last end of the chapter feature is the **Master Student Profile**. Each Master Student Profile highlights a person who embodies the qualities of a master student.

## An involving course model for classroom lesson plans

It is important to first decide on the themes and topics that you will cover in your course. Review the Table of Contents for the book you are using, and complete a textbook reconnaissance to zero in on the specific topics and articles you want to teach. Many of the strategies presented within a single topic can be used with equal effectiveness in a variety of topic sequences. The HM ClassPrep CD-ROM contains several ideas that can be used in any chapter and at any time. Keep in mind that these are only suggestions. As you design your course outline and prepare weekly or daily lesson plans, choose if, when, and where you will use these ideas.

The ideas on the HM ClassPrep CD-ROM are structured in the following seven-part format for easier application to both the planning and teaching processes. The objective is to use varying modes of instruction in order to facilitate a course that accesses and maximizes each student's method of learning. If you are more comfortable with lecture style teaching, this model will seem challenging to you at first. However, if you begin creating your lesson plans with this model as a foundation, you will find that your class is more interactive and the students will enjoy the variety that is built into this model. You can also integrate this model into other courses you might teach.

Using "An involving course model" as a framework can provide an opportunity to engage students as active participants in the learning process. The concept planning ideas are structured in this format for easier application to both the planning and teaching processes. The objective is to use varying modes of instruction in order to facility a course that accesses and maximizes each student's method of learning. The 7-part course structure looks like this:

| | |
|---|---|
| 20% | Lectures |
| 20% | Exercises |
| 20% | Conversations & sharing |
| 20% | Guest speakers & videotapes |
| 20% | Quizzes, evaluations, previews, reviews, & assignments |

Even though many college classes are often 70-90% lecture, this 7-part course structure suggests that each week in your class, whether it meets once, twice, or three times per week, that you only spend a total of only 20% of the time lecturing. Dean Mancina, Faculty Advisor for *Becoming a Master Student,* feels that one of the reasons this model works well is that the *Master Student* textbooks are so clearly written that students don't need to go over most of the tools and strategies in class.

The rest of the class meeting time, here are a list of activities that fit into a structure for a interactive class experience:
- In-class exercises
- Sharing and conversation
- Guest speakers and videotapes

If you plan each of these activities to have equal time with your lectures (about 20%), then 80% of your weekly in-class time will be filled with variety. The HM ClassPrep CD has many suggestions for applying this strategy to your course, organized by chapter and highlighting the specific activities above. Previews at the beginning of class, weekly quizzes, reviews of the material covered in the text and/or in class, and assignment of homework round out the remaining 20% of class time.

Here is an example of the application of the 7-part course structure to a lesson plan. Estimated time is in parenthesis after each item to illustrate the example for you. The following example is for a course that meets twice a week for 75 minutes each time.

**MONDAY**
Preview class agenda (4)
Collect homework (4)
Guest speaker (20)
Conversation and sharing (20)
Review of chapter reading assignment (20)
Homework and preview of next class (7)

**WEDNESDAY**
Preview Class Agenda (4)
Lecture (20)
Class Exercise (25)
Quiz (20)
Homework and Preview of next class (6)

### Writing lesson plans

Prior to each class, write your lesson plan and rehearse. Recognize the time limits and how quickly the minutes go by. Write down any announcements to be made, topics to be covered, assignments to be given, jokes or stories to be told, record-keeping procedures to be performed, answers to questions that have been asked in previous classes, or material to review before continuing. Make sure all of the material fits together.

Make a list of all of the items you will need to take to the class and check them off as you gather them together. These might include handouts, chalk, markers, 3x5 cards, pencils, two-part exercise sheets, three-part quiz sheets, student comments from the exercise or quiz collected at the last class, lecture notes, audiovisual materials, papers to return, the class attendance list, and your grade book. Be sure you have arranged for the delivery of any equipment that you or your guest speaker will need. Note how much time you expect each part of your plan to take.

Teaching sometimes resembles a theater production because it requires a great deal of preparation and attention to detail. A detailed plan allows you to have confidence, especially when you decide to deviate from it. When something unexpected happens and you choose to take advantage of the circumstances, a detailed plan allows you to quickly reprioritize and return to your plan later. A sample lesson plan follows. Plan, rehearse, be flexible, and "break a leg."

Here is another example you may choose to use as you introduce your course and the textbook.

## Student Success Course—Day 1

| | | |
|---|---|---|
| 11:00 a.m. | (3 minutes) | Welcome |
| 11:03 a.m. | (15 minutes) | Power Process "Discover what you want" |
| 11:18 a.m. | (10 minutes) | Preview using Master Student Map and "Textbook reconnaissance" exercise |
| 11:28 a.m. | (12 minutes) | "Name tag" activity<br>Purpose<br>Direction<br>Experience<br>Discussion |
| 11:40 a.m. | (15 minutes) | "Sell" class<br>Letters to new students from previous students<br>Paired discussion<br>Post office hours and phone number. |
| 11:55 a.m. | (5 minutes) | Assignment: Read and do the Introduction Chapter. Preview Chapter One |

## Student Success Course—Day 2

| | | |
|---|---|---|
| 11:00 a.m. | (3 minutes) | Welcome |
| 11:03 a.m. | (10 minutes) | Review Introduction Quiz |
| 11:13 a.m. | (30 minutes) | "Agreement" activity<br>Post office hours and phone number.<br>Give instructor's agreements<br>State expectations. |
| 11:50 a.m. | (10 minutes) | Librarian<br>Remind class of library requirement<br>Assignment: Read and do Chapter One. |

There are many ways to approach planning your course. The following are a few strategies you can use to customize your course and to construct detailed class outlines.

## 3 x 5 card course planning strategy

The purpose of using 3x5 cards for goal setting is to help teachers "divide and conquer" goals that might be difficult to attain because they seem insurmountable. These can be long- or short-term goals. In this exercise, students break these goals into tasks that can be accomplished in an hour or less.

**Part I**—Each student will need a pack of 3x5 cards for this exercise. 3X5 cards are available for free to each student who purchases a copy of a *Master* Student text from Houghton Mifflin Company. You can order your 3X5 cards from your College Survival consultant. Be sure to order them early so that they arrive by the time the first day of class comes around.

Briefly preview the directions. Brainstorm for three minutes. Tell students to think of all the things they would like to accomplish in their lives.

Give these directions: *Write each goal on a separate 3x5 card. Do this now.*

*Take a few minutes and choose one of those goals—one that will take a long time to complete, such as writing a book. For the next five to eight minutes, brainstorm again. This time, think of everything you will need to do to accomplish this goal. Write each item on a separate 3x5 card. For writing a book, your list might include the following: write it, choose a title, choose a topic, get it printed, get it published, type it, have it proofread, have it typeset, get pictures, make an outline, research. List as many different aspects of the job as you can.*

**Part II**—Time spent on the next step will vary, depending on the amount of time you have available. Fifteen minutes is a good length. You don't want to give students quite enough time to finish. This leaves them thinking about this after they leave your classroom. Encourage them to continue working on this assignment outside of class until all of the tasks can be accomplished in one hour or less. In this step, students will need some space (on the floor, a large table, a desk). Students will categorize their tasks and break down any that will take longer than one hour. They will need to make more cards to fill in the gaps. Have them lay their cards out in the shape of a pyramid and label them before picking them up. One way of labeling is to number the cards in outline form. For example, if a student has three major categories such as "Research," "Writing," and "Publishing," those cards would be labeled I, II, and III. The categories under "Research" would be labeled "IA," "IB," "IC," and so on, and cards for subcategories under the "IA" heading, for example, would be labeled "IA1," "IA2," and so forth. This labeling system will enable students to return to the task later and resume where they left off.

## Planning grid

This grid was developed by Skip Downing at Baltimore City Community College as a tool to plan each class session using an involving course model.

The sample grid provided on the next page outlines one possible way of covering material from Chapter Six: Tests.

## PLANNING GRID

| Content & Objectives | |
|---|---|
| **Test Taking** | 1. Preview & Review |
| 1. Before test: |     Use Master Student Map |
|     Manage review time |     Importance of developing test-taking strategies: |
|     Create review tools |     1.  Strategies before the test |
|     Plan a test-taking strategy |     2.  Strategies during the test |
|     Predict test questions |     3.  Strategies after the test |
|     Study groups | |
|     Stress relief activities | 2. Lecture (20%) |
| |     Study groups: Rules to make them effective: |
| 2. During test: |     1.  Regular meeting times |
|     Different types of questions |     2.  Bring 10 questions on 3x5 cards |
|     Words to watch for in essay |     3.  No socializing until all ?'s answered |
|     questions | |
| | 3. Guest Speaker (20%) |
| 3. After test: |     Health and Wellness center representative to talk |
|     Understand source of test |     about stress |
|     errors | |
|     Study incorrect answers | 4. Exercise (20%) |
| |     "Pop Quiz" |
| | |
| | 5. Conversation (20%) |
| |     Discuss "Impossible Quiz" |
| |     Discuss guest speaker |
| |     Best idea exchange |
| | |
| | 6. Assignments |
| |     Read Master Student article in Chapter Six. |
| | |
| | 7. Quiz & Evaluation |
| |     Quiz with three-part forms |
| |     Learning Styles Application (due next class meeting) |

## A word on using guest speakers

Guest speakers serve several purposes. They provide variety, present important content, and raise student awareness about available resources. Guest speakers give both you and the students a break. They take the pressure off you for a short time and expose students to different presentation styles. If there are multiple sections of your course, you can videotape guest speakers and show the videotapes to all sections. Also consider combining sections and scheduling a guest speaker so that all students can hear him. Guest speakers and the videotapes that accompany the *Master Student* texts can help you accomplish the following:

- Introduce students to campus and community resources and role models.
- Feature experts on the course content.
- Give students and instructors a change of pace.
- Showcase assistance available in the community and at the college.

Possible guest speaker formats include the following:
- Cameo appearances (15 minutes)

- Roundtable discussions with students
- Panel of speakers with moderator
- Videotapes of speakers to be shown to multiple sections of the course
- Speakers to answer any topic generated by students

## Suggestions for guest speakers from your campus and community

From on-campus:
Counselor
Career Center Coordinator
Librarian
Instructor/Department Chair from various disciplines
College President or other Administrator
Financial Aid Director
Tutor
Placement Director
Health Center Nurse
Student Government President or other representative
Residential Life coordinator

From off-campus:
Public Health Official
Professional Athlete

Women Against Violence representative
Child abuse counselor
Banker
Religious leader
Representative from local AIDS coalition
Alternative health care professional
Law enforcement official
Alcohol and substance abuse counselor
Mayor, Congressperson, or other local elected official
Alumni
Media personality or local celebrity
Rape prevention worker
Lawyer or judge
Business leader
Motivational speaker
Scientist
Mothers Against Drunk Drivers member

Sending thank-you notes to speakers gives them positive reinforcement and demonstrates your students' appreciation. You can have students write their notes on two- or three-part paper. This practice enables you to include students' handwritten comments with your own note. Also include comments from quizzes and evaluations along with student reactions to the presentation. People enjoy feedback. It can motivate them to return for the next term. Sample Thank you notes are available on the HM Class Prep CD.

## Sharing, conversation, and exercise strategies

Many of the strategies in this section apply to the logistics of class and group exercises. Students often say that being in groups is the most valuable part of the class. It is a time when you turn the class content over to students, inviting their comments, observations, and discoveries. It is your turn to listen.

During conversations and sharing, students usually become more aware of similarities in their experiences. We often assume that no one shares our struggles, joys, troubles, questions, and concerns. Through conversations and sharing, students learn that others have the same fears, worries, strengths, and goals. They often discover that they are not alone in the challenges they face.

Students can begin to bond with other students and develop a personal support system. They can let their classmates know of their needs for childcare, rides, or help in certain subject areas. The more supportive relationships a student has, the more likely he will persist and achieve his educational goals.

Conversations and sharing also allow students to get to know the instructor and to voice opinions and concerns. Instructors who are informed about student needs and issues can be valuable advocates for them and can convey such concerns to the administration.

Having to speak in front of others is one of the strongest fears many of us have. Asking questions and participating in class discussions are important—and sometimes necessary—skills for students to develop. When a safe, structured environment has been created that promotes public speaking, students often report moving beyond their fears about speaking in class.

Sharing and Conversation activities can include the following:
- Discovery of common concerns and celebrations
- Discovery of potential support groups by hearing about others' experiences
- "Dress rehearsal" for speaking in other classes
- "Thinking out loud" without debate Alternate titles for these activities might invite greater participation:
- "Comparing notes"
- "Comments or questions"
- "Your turn"
- "Temperature-taking"
- "Open microphone"
- "Quotable quotations"

Here are some guidelines to help generate valuable sharing experiences for students.

**Model sharing.** If you are willing to share parts of yourself that the average student does not see, you become more human in the eyes of your students. They will probably be more willing to share their insecurities, questions, dreams, achievements, or challenges with someone who is "real" to them.

**Allow time for silence.** Students often need some time to think before they know what they want to say or before they have the courage to say it. Allowing silence is essential in creating an atmosphere that says, "Your ideas are important to me. I am willing to let you have time to think so that I can hear what is happening with you." Explaining this concept to students is appropriate since they are probably not used to having instructors give them much time to think before they talk. The recommendation here is to wait 30 seconds or more before breaking the silence. Make sure your body language matches your message of inviting students to speak. Be relaxed. Since silence is uncomfortable for many people, this might take some practice.

Let the students know that the silence isn't intended to pressure anyone or make them feel guilty for not talking. Rather, it is to give them time to look inside themselves to see if they have anything to contribute or reveal.

**Listen with detachment.** Conversations and sharing is a time when students sometimes vent their frustrations and voice their complaints. If a student talks about something you might take personally, listen without rebuttal, justification, or defense. Frequently, just feeling safe and having someone listen attentively is solution enough for students.

**Have "seeds" available.** Sometimes, inspirational stories, moving poems, meaningful songs, questions about the value of course material, or comments about school and community events trigger talking. Questions about current events, politics, environmental concerns, or even how Student Success techniques have been useful in other areas of students' lives are appropriate. Anonymously reading Discovery and Intention Statements that you have collected from students often generates useful conversations.

Here are some possible "seeds":
- What are your reactions to the film [or exercise or guest speaker]?
- Find two items in your purse, wallet, or pocket that are important to you. Talk about them.
- Which ideas or techniques from the book have you tried? Which ones worked? Which ones didn't work?
- What do you need from your family or friends to promote your success?
- How can the faculty or administration of the school promote your success?
- What are some of your obstacles to getting what you want from school?
- What exciting or interesting things are happening around the school or community?
- What interesting occurrence in your life would you like to talk about?
- Describe a time when you were successful.
- What advice would you give to a new student?
- What if you applied a strategy that you are learning in this class to one of your other courses? How do you think it would work?
- What if you applied these strategies from class to your job or your intended career? How do you think they would apply?

**Change the physical environment.** Sometimes a change in the physical of environment helps cue conversations or exercises. For example, have students pull their desks into a circle or semicircle, or have them all stand up or sit on the floor. Getting them out of their passive listening-to-a-lecture posture could encourage more receptivity and openness.

**Structure the time.** Try this technique developed by Virginia Satir, a world-renowned author, lecturer, and counselor. She calls it "Temperature Taking." Once during each class period, announce that it's time for Temperature Taking. This is an opportunity to find out what is going on with people in the room. It is when you listen to students in a loving, nonjudgmental way. List the following five items on the blackboard and then discuss each one. Give anyone in the room a chance to speak at each step of the way. If no one has a comment, move to the next item. If this exercise tends to take too long, set a time limit before you start. The five steps to guide the sharing are: (1) appreciations, (2) bugs, (3) puzzles, (4) new information, and (5) hopes and wishes.

When introducing the idea of Temperature Taking, let the students know the ground rules for each of the steps. The guideline for appreciations ("warm fuzzies") is that they be specific. Compliment the details of what you like rather than giving general praise.

Irritations are expressed during the second step, bugs. When complaining, a student must also present three possible solutions. The group can then offer additional solutions. Puzzles are questions; in this third step, the group is invited to give answers to the perplexed person or at least to describe ways to find an answer.

Step four, new information, is the time to relate anything new that has happened. In step five, hopes and wishes are limited to those of the person speaking. This is not a time to wish someone else were different. The group is asked to do all it can do to make the person's wish come true.

**Relax and have fun.** This is a time when you can get to know the students in your class, and they can get to know you. It can be rewarding for everyone.

## Discuss Guidelines for conversations and sharing

It is helpful to discuss the guidelines for conversations and sharing on the first or second day of class. It is important to let students know what you expect. Students are more willing to participate when the environment is safe, and knowing the ground rules increases their feelings of safety.

Any topic can be brought up during conversations and sharing. The suggested approach is holistic because all aspects of our lives are interrelated. An exciting or disturbing event in one area of a student's life will carry over into all other areas, even if only in a minor way. If you are uncomfortable about allowing certain subjects to be raised, you can restrict this guideline by directing the students to share anything related to school.

Confidentiality is essential in providing a safe atmosphere for sharing. Ask students to agree that anything discussed in the classroom during conversations and sharing stays there. This dictum cannot be enforced, yet it is important to request and emphasize it.

Sometimes students' comments about themselves, about you, about others, or about the institution will be negative. If the problem mentioned is about a specific person, request that no names be used. This policy can be useful for keeping this activity from turning into a mudslinging or person-bashing session.

## Lectures

In the "Lectures" sections throughout the HM ClassPrep CD-ROM, you will find suggestions for various lectures appropriate for this course. It is difficult for most instructors to limit lectures to 20 percent of class time. Even when we know that lecturing is not the most effective teaching tool, we might be influenced by our own experiences as students and by the joy of being "on stage." Also, for some teachers, lecturing is far easier than attempting to get students to participate more actively in the class. In order to maximize the effectiveness of lectures and to avoid reliance on them, keep the following objectives in mind:

- Highlight material for students and encourage them to discover the content.
- Draw relationships among topics in the areas of academic and workplace skills.
- Explain the transferability of skills to other disciplines.
- Address predictable student crisis phases before they occur.
- For a "last lecture," decide what you most want to say to students completing your course.

Allow students to learn the basic content of the class from the text. Lectures can then be used to re-emphasize and clarify content, or to introduce new or supplemental material.

Give lectures over areas in which you have special skills and in which the students show interest. For instance, you might be an armchair specialist in nutrition and cognizant of how nutrition, food sensitivities, and vitamins affect academic performance. If so, a lecture about what you know might be entertaining and educational. Perhaps you were a professional speechwriter for ten years prior to your teaching career. You might want to spend more time and energy on the Reading or Notes chapters. Your enthusiasm for a subject that engages you will be contagious and in turn can help keep students' interest high.

Lecturing for re-emphasis can be tricky because students don't want to be treated as if they aren't smart enough to figure out what's in the book. However, when reading the text, students sometimes skim over or even totally dismiss important concepts and techniques without a second thought.

Lecturing about critical ideas is one way to encourage that second thought. Often it is sufficient to say, "Yes, the nine steps of Muscle Reading seem like a lot of work, and I want to discuss them with you briefly because I am convinced that they will save you hours of rereading time. I did a lot of rereading before tests when I was a student, and it wasn't any fun!" Using a personal example or story is a good way to re-emphasize an important point.

Selling the benefits of using the strategies presented in the text increases the likelihood that students will experiment with them. Lectures about how student success skills can transfer to careers can make students aware of other applications for them. The Put it to Work feature (or Career Applications) in the text will support this effort.

If students are confused about an idea or a technique, you might find it useful to give lectures to clarify material after quizzes or class discussions. These lectures might seem more like class discussions because you will need feedback to figure out what is confusing students and how you can best re-explain ideas to make them understandable.

## Assignments

The journal entries, exercises, and other written activities in the *Master Student* text are designed to help the student see the application of the tool or concept to their own life. It's important that students complete as many of these written exercises in the book as possible. One strategy to ensure that students use the book as interactively as possible, while keeping instructor grading time to a reasonable level, is to require that the students complete all of the written exercises and activities in the book within the assigned homework reading pages. When the students come to class, randomly select one of the exercises to be turned in. The pages of *Master Student* are perforated for easy removal. That way, the students must complete all exercises, and you will only have to grade one exercise each week. When you return the assignment, students can put the page deep in the binding where it belongs, and it will stay there.

Or, you may prefer to assign specific written exercises within the text homework assignment each week. Remember to check out the additional homework assignments that are available online at the Master Student Website (http://masterstudent.college.hmco.com) for additional options.

### Lesson Plans and Learning Styles

Writing lesson plans around the cycle of learning is a method of teaching that reaches all students—no matter what their learning style is. The Master Student Map that begins each chapter and the Learning Styles Application are two ways that you can begin to incorporate Learning Styles into your lesson plans. Begin by having students read (or re-read) the Master Student Map at the beginning of class. Challenge them to think about *why* the think the chapter is important, to them. Ask them *what* they would like to take away from this chapter and *how* they intend to practice the new skills. Introduce *what if* questions by asking students to ask themselves *What if* I apply these strategies in my other courses, at my workplace, or in my personal life.

Conclude each chapter by having your students complete the Learning Styles Application. These exercises have all been revised to help your students "cycle" through the four styles, or modes, of learning. By practicing using this learning cycle, students can begin to establish a pattern for thinking—in this course and others. Models of the cycle of learning in action are on page LSI-2 of the student text.

Using Kolb's learning styles model, the cycle begins with a concrete experience of a learning event or experience. Students reflect on this learning event, then create concepts from the event, and finally actively experiment or try out the learning event. This cyclical approach provides all learners with an opportunity to demonstrate their most developed skills at least 25 percent of the time. This also means that they will struggle some of the time and will have opportunities to learn new skills.

**Mode 1 of the learning process**—combining concrete experience with reflective observation. Your lesson plan begins by laying the groundwork or establishing the context for what is to come. Talk about the content in general terms while giving many concrete "daily life" examples. The purpose of using such examples is to help students connect the new content with something they have already experienced, thus making the content more meaningful. Discussion time can be useful for encouraging students to learn more.

**Mode 2 of the learning process**—combining reflective observation and abstract conceptualization. Now begin to lecture or provide the specific content of the lesson plan. This is when students begin to comprehend the material and start creating concepts that form new building blocks of learning. They begin to put the pieces of the whole together as the facts are presented to them.

**Mode 3 of the learning process**—combining abstract conceptualization and active experimentation. Your role now is to coach students' experimentation with the content. This is when students can determine whether the content will be useful to them. You can either do activities or exercises in the classroom or give outside assignments. These activities can be individualized or done in small groups. Students will be more active at this stage, and you will be coaching and facilitating.

**Mode 4 of the learning process**—combining active experimentation and concrete experience. As students are actively experimenting with the content and discovering its utility in their lives, you can help them evaluate their results. At this stage, students integrate the content into their behavior and add something of them to it. In other words, they can now talk about the content in general terms and provide several "daily life" concrete examples of their own.

All learners have certain skills that assist or augment their ability to be successful in the classroom. Following is a list of activities that best facilitate each mode of learning. You can check your lesson plans to see if they include options, activities, and approaches that provide all learners with the opportunity to excel in your class. Use the list below as a guide.

**Preferred learning activities**

Mode 1 Learners
Motivational stories
Journal writing
Simulations
Subjective tests
Group problem solving
Socratic lecture
Role playing

Mode 2 Learners
Formal lectures
Library searches
Textbook reading

Objective tests
Problem solving by instructor
Lectures with visual aids
Independent research

Mode 3 Learners
Homework problems
Lectures with demonstrations
Guided labs
Objective tests
Example problems worked by students
Computer-aided instruction
Individual reports

26

Mode 4 Learners
Open-ended problems
Quality circles
Open-ended labs
Subjective tests
Problems prepared by students
Student lectures
Student presentations
A lesson plan for teaching time management follows, noting the preferred learning activities of the four learners' styles.

## Mode 1 Learners' Goal: making a personal connection with the content

- Ask questions such as: "Have you ever needed more time to do all that you wanted to do? Would you like to know how to get more done in less time?"
- Role-play situations from your own life or from your students' lives to illustrate how you or they currently manage time.
- Ask students to write Discovery and Intention Statements about their use of time (to take a First Step about time).
- Ask students to write a response paper on "If I had all the time in the world, I would. . . ."

## Mode 2 Learners' Goal: gathering information about various systems of time management

- Ask students to discuss in small groups their current methods of managing time (both positive and negative) and to list all of the methods.
- Next, reconvene the class as a large group and share all of the methods that students use to manage time.
- Give this assignment: "Monitor your time for one time period (day, weekend, week), using any method you prefer, and log your activities."
- Teach concepts of time management from *Becoming a Master Student*: the Time Monitor/Time Plan, 25 ways to get the most out of now, and the seven-day antiprocrastination plan.

## Mode 3 Learners' Goal: learning new concepts and applying them

- Continue teaching concepts such as the ABC daily to-do's priority system and goal setting.
- Complete this in-class exercise: "Now that you have monitored your time and have learned some new concepts and strategies, plan and monitor your next day, weekend, or week."
- Discuss (in small groups and as a large group) the discoveries students made after completing this exercise.

## Mode 4 Learners Goal: refining the applications and applying the learning

- Present mini-lectures on the Power Process "Be here now," goal setting, and the Master Student Profile.
- Ask students to write about their goals (academic, personal, and career).
- Ask students to role-play, make posters, or use music to demonstrate effective time-management skills.
- Ask students to write themselves a letter about their commitment to use more effective time-management techniques; place it in a self-addressed, stamped envelope; and hand it in. Mail these letters back to students in six months.
- Ask students to begin teaching to fellow students, family, and friends what they have learned about time management.

## Quizzes and evaluations

Quizzes and evaluations can help you accomplish the following:
- Emphasize the rigor of this and other college courses
- Provide feedback for instructor and student
- Encourage teaching toward objectives
- Facilitate practice and application of skills
- Provide information useful for improving the quality of the course

Quizzes provide feedback to instructors and students and are consistent with higher education curriculum design and practices. They are valuable in determining how students are comprehending, applying, and experiencing the material being presented in the course. Content-related questions can be balanced with questions asking students to give their affective reactions to the course. Quizzes can tell you which ideas need clarification, which techniques could use re-emphasis, and how the overall atmosphere and content of the class can be improved. Compliments and complaints can be passed along (anonymously, of course) to those administrators and staff members most involved in the areas discussed.

If a large number of students miss a specific content question, consider reviewing that material in class. If students rave about a particular guest speaker, consider inviting him back again.

Quizzes can be short. Five or six questions take about 10 to 15 minutes to complete.

Generalizing about student reactions based on the comments of only a few is tempting and dangerous. Using quizzes and evaluations to find out exactly how many students think and feel can help you decide what adjustments, if any, to make.

# Teaching your Student Success course

Once you have an understanding of the format of the textbook, and the involving course model, this section will begin to help you to teach your course. Specific syllabi and exercises for the textbook you are using are available on the HM ClassPrep CD for your book, and are further supported by the Master Student website at http://masterstudent.college.hmco.com.

## Classroom Management and Troubleshooting

*This section presents ideas for handling common problems that might surface for many teachers of Student Success courses. These suggestions have worked for others. Nevertheless, your own intuition and creativity in handling classroom situations will be far more valuable than trying to copy someone else's style. As with everything in this manual, adapt and modify these suggestions to fit your needs and presentation style.*

If you have specific concerns that you would like to discuss with an experienced Student Success professional, consider calling upon your College Survival consultant. Your consultant can be reached at 800-528-8323 or via e-mail at collegesurvival@hmco.com. Consultants are higher education educators and/or administrators who enjoy the opportunity to strategize with you and co-create options for success in your classroom.

### Strategies for addressing students who resist the class

Sometimes students resist taking this course. This is especially true if the program is new, required, or perceived as developmental. Here are a few suggestions for dealing with resistance.

**"Sell" the course**—At the beginning of the class, "sell" the students on the benefits they will receive from the course. Talk about how you think it is valuable, what the school philosophy is, and what they can gain academically and personally. One way to do this is using the Discovery Wheel. An example of this use the Discovery Wheel to sell your course is available on your HM Class Prep CD. Look for "The Discovery Wheel" in Chapter 1, and also "If the Discovery Wheel did not convince them..." for additional ideas and strategies.

**Recognize room for improvement**—Surprisingly, A students often seem to get the most out of student success techniques and speak most highly of the course. They want to study more effectively in less time. Students who protest that they "made it through high school" probably have a lot of room for improvement. Those students who really are satisfied with their study techniques will find that learning about themselves, each other, school policies, and resources while participating in the course is a worthwhile benefit.

**Point to transferability**—Many of the techniques students learn in this class are the same ones that will help your students build successful careers, form happy relationships, and improve the quality of their lives. One way to begin a discussion about transferable skills is using the materials in the Introduction of your text. Discover what you want, a Power Process in the Introduction, also highlights the power of discovery and transferability. If you are using *Becoming a Master Student, Eleventh Edition, Becoming a Master Student Athlete,* or *Becoming a Master Student, Canadian Fourth Edition,* begin each class lesson with the Put it to Work article that appears at the end of the chapter. If you are using one of these textbooks but feel that your students would benefit from a more thorough conversation about transferable skills, ask your consultant to send you a desk copy of *From Master Student to Master Employee.* This text highlights the transferability of workplace and classroom skills with each article and example. While this book is effective for any first year student course, it may be most interesting to returning students, adult learners and students attending college for a certificate that they will immediately apply to getting a better job (or keeping their existing job).

**Distinguish between "liking" and "benefiting"**—We don't always like that which benefits us. Most students find something to dislike about the class. At the same time, it is almost certain that there will be beneficial aspects. Even if students find only a few ideas that work for them, their performance can still improve significantly. Those who resist the class and allow what they don't like to keep them from realizing its benefits are cheating themselves.

**Be firm**—Be clear about the guidelines for your class. Tell the students what you expect. If, after you do your best to convince them of the advantages of participating in class, some students choose to disrupt class and ignore your guidelines, it is appropriate to ask them to leave. If they complain that the course is required, tell them that you will not allow disruptive behavior in your class and that they must follow the guidelines or they will have to leave and repeat the course another term or not graduate. There is no reason to allow disruptive behavior in your class.

**Bring in a speaker**—Invite course alumni to your classroom to discuss how they benefited from taking your course, and how they are currently using what they learned from it. Sophomore students make excellent speakers, but also consider inviting junior and senior level students. Each can share different types of knowledge and mentor your first year students.

**Collect and read anonymous evaluations**—Ask students to answer several questions about their reactions to the course on two-part sheets of paper. Possible questions include "What is effective and what is ineffective about this class?" and "What would make this course more worthwhile for you?" Also ask students to describe which methods and strategies they have found to be helpful and which have not worked. Read both positive and negative comments. During the first few class sessions, you can use comments from students who took the course previously. Later, you can share comments from students currently enrolled.

**Do your own evaluation**—Step back and look at the course from the vantage point of a student. If you were a student in your class, would you be getting what you need to reach your goals? Are the lectures, exercises, and other classroom activities assisting students in mastering the course objectives as stated in the syllabus? After you have thoughtfully evaluated your course, be willing to change. Telling students about the results of your evaluation and the changes you will make models a powerful way of taking risks and learning from mistakes. If you conclude that you are doing a good job, continue with confidence. Your job is to provide an opportunity for students to teach themselves.

## Strategies for addressing students who are not reading the textbook
**Test over the reading**—The text is designed to give students the content of the course. If they don't read and use the book, they aren't getting the most value for their money. Giving quizzes in class over the assigned material will encourage reading. Here's a simple quiz format: ask your students to write *why* they felt the article (or materials you've assigned) are important; ask your students to identify *what* the most important part of the article was to them; ask your students *how* they intend to apply these skills; and ask your students to predict the results *if* they apply the technique or skill to a specific course.

**Collect exercises and Journal Entries**—When you give a reading assignment, tell students that you will collect one of the exercises in the text. Don't tell them which one. Because the students won't know which exercise you will ask for, they might be more motivated to complete all of them.

Some of the exercises request absolute honesty from students. If students suspect you will choose one of these exercises, they might not participate with the fullest level of personal integrity. You can tell students which exercises you definitely will *not* collect and why (which will likely pique their curiosity).

Ask quiz questions about the exercises and Journal Entries—whether you collect exercises and Journal Entries or not, ask questions about them on your quizzes. If students know that they will be asked about the exercises and Journal Entries, they are more likely to complete them. Questions could be about students' personal discoveries and possible applications of what they have learned.

**Collect the quizzes**—The process of writing quiz answers will be beneficial, even if the student only paraphrases the answers from the articles or works with another student to complete the answers. When students know that quizzes will have to be removed from the text and turned in, they are more likely to read actively and invest more energy in learning the material. They will also realize that they are expected to participate actively with the text. This includes removing and reinserting pages, writing in the margins, and doing the exercises. Using the text in these ways will increase the book's value for the students.

**Allow students to teach**—Teaching is one of the best ways to learn. Since most students are not confident enough in their speaking skills to stand up and "wing it," they will probably be motivated to prepare before they teach. Consequently, they will learn the material they are about to present. Students might also gain an appreciation for your efforts as an instructor.

**Tailor the text**—Select the articles and exercises most appropriate for your class. Keep your course purpose and objectives in mind when you decide what to keep and what to omit. There are likely too many articles and exercises in the book for you and your students to review all of them. Remember that it is okay to select certain pieces and leave the others for students to discover on their own.

## Strategies for addressing students who say they do not need this course

**Complete the Discovery Wheel**—The Discovery Wheel in Chapter 1 is an opportunity for students to think about the kind of student they are and the kind of student they want to become. The Discovery Wheel previews all of the topics covered in the text, and illustrates the skill level each student has for each of the sections. Highlight for students the Discover Wheel in the last chapter of the text. This will help students assess their progress from the beginning of your course to the end of the semester.

**Agree with them**—Acknowledge that students probably already know a great deal about being successful. Also acknowledge that there is always room for improvement. Ask students to consider the possibility that learning and adopting a few truly effective strategies can save them time, improve their performance, and make a significant difference in the quality of their school experiences.

**Use course alumni as guest speakers**—Students listen attentively to other students. You can often find alumni who resisted the course at first and later on became great proponents of it.

**Celebrate small achievements**—Very few of us ever have an opportunity to improve 100 percent. Suggest that improving 1 percent in a hundred different ways can accomplish an equally impressive result.

## Strategies for working with students who are failing your course

**Hold a conference**—Set aside time for a face-to-face talk about your expectations and the student's expectations for the class. There might be confusion about what is required. Often homework is neglected due to other difficulties in a student's life. A committed listener is sometimes all that is needed. If more help with assignments is appropriate, refer students to other resources, such as the campus peer tutoring program.

**Remind students**—Review the requirements for passing the course. The HM Class Prep CD provides you with a "contract" template that you can have students sign. Reminding students about their contract and commitment to your course can help to refocus failing students. Procrastination can be deadly—even for A students.

**Detach**—Allow students to make their own decisions and to accept the consequences. Students should take responsibility for their choices. Beware of your desire to take care of them. Some students will choose to fail. Failing this class can be a valuable experience. If a student fails accounting, she can say, "I never was very good at math." If she fails creative writing, she might complain, "I had a poor second-grade teacher." However, if she fails a Student Success course, she has the opportunity to admit that she simply chose to fail.

**Examine your standards**—Determine whether or not you have set realistic goals for the class. If 50 percent of the class does not comprehend the material, examine your teaching methods, testing style, and classroom atmosphere. Feedback from students in the form of anonymous evaluations can be helpful, even if a little painful. If you decide that the way you are handling the class is satisfactory (remember, there is always room for improvement), then detach. Having students who choose to fail your class does not make you a bad person or a poor teacher. Talk with other instructor's on your campus to learn how they've mastered teaching a difficult subject. Call your College Survival consultant, or look on the HM ClassPrep CD for more ideas for teaching.

## Strategies for addressing students who feel insulted
**Acknowledge their skills**—Students possess valuable life experiences that can assist them in school. This class can help them translate and adapt those skills in ways that will promote their success.

**Let them choose**—Have students pick and choose what's important for them. Encourage them to use the content that is applicable to them. Students can even select the order in which your class use the text. Perhaps test-taking skills are important to your students. Consider teaching this material after Chapter 1. Each of the chapters stand alone in such a way that this will not disrupt backtracking to chapters you've skipped.

**Focus on special challenges**—Different students face unique and different challenges. Define and discuss these challenges in class. Consider collecting Discovery Wheels to determine which topics are most relevant to your specific students. If their needs are in an area where you feel you are not an expert (like financial planning, or health issues) invite a guest speaker to class.

**Share the truth**—Explain that your students have a diverse range of skills. While you don't want to insult those who already know some of these concepts, for those who don't, this is the course in which they will hear and learn them. When a student hears something they already know, instead of taking the attitude that this information is a waste of their time, they might celebrate this as a student success strategy they already have so don't need to learn how to use and to practice.

## Strategies for addressing the feeling that students seem to dislike you
**Don't jump to conclusions**—Sometimes the most unresponsive-looking students are creating an incredible amount of value for themselves from the course materials.

**Don't give up**—Some students have a cool or tough act that takes a while to break through.

32

**Don't take it personally**—Of the more than five billion people in the world, some won't like you no matter what you do. Remember the distinction between "liking" and "benefiting." They don't have to like you to learn from you. Refer to the article "Create your instructor" in the text for a more complete discussion of this concept.

**Remember your purpose**—Your job is to promote student success, not to win a popularity contest. Being the person who holds up a mirror of self-responsibility and holds students accountable is not always a popular role. Sometimes you must choose between being liked and doing your job.

## Strategies for addressing students who exhibit disruptive behaviors

**Be clear about your rules**—Set limits and enforce them. Consistency is important. Students sometimes test teachers to find out where the lines are drawn. A practice of enforcing the rules one day and letting them slide the next is confusing to students. Be explicit about your expectations and be consistent about applying the consequences for not following the rules.

**Ask students to remember their purpose**—Ask students to reflect on their reasons for being in school and what they hope to gain. Discuss side conversations and have students consider the costs and benefits of such behavior.

**Give feedback**—Use "I" messages to share your observations, feelings, thoughts, wants, and intentions about side conversations. The purpose is to communicate in a way that students understand, not to make them feel defensive.

**Stop talking**—Your silence is usually enough to get the students' attention.

**Contract with students**—Include "no side conversations" as one of the agreements in the "Agreements and the student agreement contract" exercise.

**Don't allow it**—Even though you might give students a choice on the "Agreement contract" exercise and some might not agree to stop having side conversations, you don't have to tolerate talking in your class. Decide on your policy ahead of time and state it. While you cannot physically stop side conversations, you can enforce consequences. One or two reminders will usually handle the problem. If this approach doesn't work, ask students who are disruptive to sit apart from each other. If class participation is part of a student's grade, points can be deducted for side conversations. If students continue to have side conversations, request that they leave the room. Students then know that if they choose to have side conversations, they are choosing to be dismissed from the classroom.

**Claim your classroom space**—Walk around the classroom as you present material. Standing next to students who are having side conversations as you continue to present material lets them know that side conversations are not acceptable in your class.

**Establish guidelines for and reinforce acceptable behavior**—Include on the syllabus a written statement of the kind of behavior that contributes to a productive learning environment.

**Immediately engage the student**—Speak the name of the disruptive student while asking her to contribute or respond to what is being presented or discussed in class at the time.

**Document continued disruptions**—Keep dated notes regarding a student's behavior and ask to meet with the student. Be ready to make a referral to counseling or student services, if it is appropriate.

**Change testing conditions**—Separate students. Have student assistants monitor the class during tests.

**Allow students to work in teams**—Working in teams encourages camaraderie and support groups. Students can study together, take the test together, and receive a group grade. You can design tests that require some group discussion and group decision making.

## Strategies for encouraging more class participation from your students

**Review the advantages of full participation**—Discuss what students will gain, what obstacles to their success they might overcome, and how each exercise relates to the purpose of the course. Ask them to consider how much more they learn when they risk feeling foolish.

**Be structured**—Give highly structured directions that lead students through exercises step by step. Sometimes having to discuss a topic with others or even having to choose a partner frightens students. Use specific directions such as: "In a moment stand up, walk around the room, and ask people when they were born. When you find someone born during the same month as you, find a place to sit down with that person. You can sit anywhere in the classroom. Then, exchange names and have a brief conversation. I will then give you the next directions. Now, stand up and pick a partner."

**Demonstrate**—Use volunteers or model what is expected. Demonstrate the whole exercise, if necessary, to clarify what it requires and to help students feel more comfortable with it.

**Give them the choice**—Students who choose not to participate have as much to learn about themselves as those who do take part. You can still ask students who do not participate to write Discovery Statements and Intention Statements about what they learned by not participating.

## Strategies for addressing students who do not attend class

**Call them**—Be sure that your records include a telephone number or an address for each student. A contact works best if it is made in a completely non-threatening way. Avoid being judgmental. The purpose of this course is to encourage each student to succeed according to her definition of success. Remind the student of your purpose and express your concern about her performance.

**Invite them to contact you**—Recommend that students stop by your office. An interested teacher is often all that is needed to get a student back on track.

## Strategies for addressing students who complain that they do not have time

**Suggest the opposite**—Tell students that they can't afford not to have time for the course work. Taking this course can dramatically improve their efficiency and therefore give them more time for other things.

**Discuss the benefits**—The benefits from this class will carry over into all of the students' other classes and into the rest of their lives. Investing their time and energy can pay off in higher grades, more efficient use of time and money, better relationships, and so on.

**Give synergistic assignments**—Design your assignments so that students can combine them with assignments for other classes. For example, have students use Muscle Reading for their history assignment. They could submit to you an outline, questions that they generated before they read the assignment, and the answers to those questions. They could also write an evaluation of the effectiveness of the strategy as an assignment.

**Remind students of the transferability of skills**—Your students can apply the skills they learn in the classroom to different parts of their life, whether they are spending time with their family or at their workplace. Have your students write Journal Entries about how they discover the application of your course material to the rest of their lives. This will help them to make intentions to be successful in your course.

### Strategies for addressing students who complain that the text is too expensive

**Encourage students to keep the text**—Describe the text as an owner's manual for an expensive purchase called "education." Encourage students to keep the text after the course ends as a resource manual for the rest of their education. Writing a speech might not be a concern until their fourth term. If they still have the text, they can review the speechwriting suggestions then.

**Consider the value of information**—Even if students adopt only two or three ideas from the hundreds that are suggested in the text, those ideas can make a significant difference in their performance in school and beyond. The investment in improving their school performance and the resulting impact on the rest of their lives are far more valuable than the cost of the text.

**Shop around**—Bookstores have different percentages of markup. Alternatives to buying through the college bookstore might be available. Be sure to get permission from the appropriate people. You can also discuss the markup with your bookstore manager and request that the store maintain reasonable prices.

**Compare prices**—Compare the cost of *Master Student* to the prices of similarly formatted books in other disciplines. Students will find this text competitively priced.

**Encourage active participation**—The value of the text is increased when students actively participate with it. Stress that *Master Student* is a text. The assignments are not simply to "read" the chapters; rather, students are expected to "read and do" them. Be sure that exercises and quizzes are completed and turned in to you.

**Make informed decisions**—Find out the extent of the concerns about the text's price. Often a vocal minority gets more attention than the rest of the students. When you know the extent of the problem, you can make more effective decisions about how to handle it.

**Offer scholarships**—Create a scholarship fund for students with special needs. Direct students to financial resources that already exist or suggest other possibilities that they can explore.

**Prioritize your lesson on managing money**—Sometimes students who say they can't afford to purchase the text might be experiencing other financial problems. The suggestions in the Planning chapter can help students discover other places to find money. The exercises on the HMClassPrep CD-ROM can also help students improve their money management. Have students compare the cost of the text to the costs of other commonly purchased items and discuss the relative value of each to their lives and education.

**Highlight benefits**—Ask students to consider the impact the course can have on their success in school and, consequently, on their success in life. Generating a list of all of the benefits can help reinforce their decision to take the course. These lists can be offered to administrators to help expand the course and to give students credit for taking it.

**Petition your school**—Do public relations work for the course. Go through appropriate procedures and channels to express your thoughts about the importance of the course, what it has to offer students, and how the institution will benefit. Campaign for the course to be made available to everyone for credit so that there is a reward for students in addition to that of self-improvement.

**Consider transcript credit**—Credit can sometimes appear on the students' transcripts and not be applied toward their degrees or calculated into their GPAs. This can be a workable compromise for schools with complicated credit-granting policies.

## Strategies for receiving help if your course lacks support

**Contact College Survival**—College Survival can assist you in gaining faculty and administrative support for your course. Call 800-528-8323 and ask to speak with one of the educational consultants or to arrange an on-site training at your college.

**Outline the benefits**—Describe the expected results of the course to administrators. When a successful course is delivered, students, faculty, administrators, and staff all benefit. Your HM ClassPrep CD has a special section entitled "Gaining Support." This section highlights how to enroll faculty and administrators in creating a framework on your campus.

**Use past evaluations**—Testimonials from students who have taken the class can help your colleagues see the benefits of this course. You can also videotape students discussing their reactions to the course. Administrators might be more willing to watch a short videotape than to read dozens of written evaluations. Another possibility is to summarize evaluations, quoting pertinent and typical comments.

**Conference call**—Set up a conference call with a consultant from College Survival. Invite anyone who might be interested in, involved with, or skeptical about the Student Success course to participate.

**Share retention figures**—Tracking retention rates will supply the evidence you need to convince others about the value of the course. More information about collecting retention information on your campus is in the Course Manual and on your HM ClassPrep CD.

**Send letters**—Send letters to all faculty, advisors, and administrators describing the course and its purpose. Invite anyone who is interested to sit in on a class or to be a guest speaker.

**Offer workshops**—Schedule workshops on course content. Many of your colleagues might be interested in time management, goal setting, interpersonal communications, or the Power Processes.

## Strategies for instructors who have little time to prepare

Sometimes the assignment to teach a Student Success course is given only days before the course begins. This circumstance is unfortunate and ineffective, and not hopeless. Two of the *Master Student* texts have Annotated Instructor's Editions (AIEs): *Becoming a Master Student, Eleventh Edition* and *From Master Student to Master Employee.* The resources in these Annotated Instructor's Editions are designed to help instructors immediately use the textbook and effectively teach the new material to their students. The Master Instructor Resource Guide that is a part of the AIE outlines ancillary resources that are available. Here are some addition suggestions that can help.

**Seek assistance**—Instructors who have taught the course before are often willing to assist you. Ask them to help you get started.

**Use this Course Manual**—Do a textbook reconnaissance of the Course Manual first to get the big picture. Focus on your course purpose first. Then, when you have more time, explore the rest of the manual to develop a more solid foundation from which to create a successful course.

**Enlist student support**—Ask students to help you prioritize what's important to them. See the exercise called "Co-creating a syllabus" on the HMClassPrep CD-ROM.

**Do preventive work for next time**—Describe the problems resulting from not having had sufficient preparation time. Point to the costs for students, for instructors, and for the institution itself. Request that future instructors be given enough time to prepare for this class. Stress that when the class is supported and delivered effectively, retention rates improve and everybody wins.

**Call College Survival**—The consultants at College Survival have dealt with almost every problem imaginable related to Student Success courses. Whatever your situation, they are likely to have a variety of suggestions and/or resources to share. Call 800-528-8323.

## Strategies for encouraging course enrollment

**Market the course**—Use brochures, newspaper articles, letters to parents and spouses, T-shirts, orientation speeches, letters to advisors, letters to students, and posters to describe the benefits of the course.

At a Student Success Course Workshop in Charleston, SC, participants conducted a brainstorm session on ways to promote a Student Success course to students. They compiled the following list during the session as a springboard for creating other innovative ideas. Look through this list of ideas. What could you adopt or adapt to promote your course?

- Have the class create a mascot and a song.
- Use a hot air balloon to advertise the course.
- Publicize course results in faculty and student newspapers.
- Ask current students to write a newsletter article about the course for extra credit.
- Feature the "master students" in the course in a newsletter or on a bulletin board.
- Have a bring-a-friend-to-class day.
- Send out course information with admissions packets.
- Give local store and restaurant discounts to students who take the course.
- Award a prize to the student who directs the most referrals to the course.
- Create a master students' club for course graduates.
- Give special T-shirts away to the graduates of the class.
- Have a lottery for a free book and tuition credit for those who register.
- Perform a skit at orientation about the course.
- Bake a cake for registration that looks like the text and says, "Have a piece of success."
- Have successful course graduates attend registration wearing a button or sign that identifies them.
- Preprint the course title and number on registration cards.

**Enlist help**—Enlist advisors, registration and admissions staff, and others to help promote the course to students.

**Schedule the class at prime times**—A class offered at 5:30 p.m. on Friday is not considered a viable option for many students. Request that your course be scheduled at a reasonable time.

## Strategies for addressing the amount of material to cover

*Master Student* was not designed to offer a prescription on how to be successful. It covers a wide range of topics and contains hundreds of suggestions that require experimentation by individual students to discover what they need and what is effective for them.

**Pick and choose**—Don't cover it all. Select only those items that are most useful. Get students' input to help you prioritize. Covering the most important items in depth might be more useful than trying to present all the material.

**Assign extra credit**—Students who may fall behind during the semester are often interested in trying to "make up" points or grades. Suggest students read articles and write Discovery and Intention statements from a part of a chapter you did not assign. Or consider assigning additional exercises for them to complete.

**Suggest keeping the text**—Students can keep their texts throughout their college years. When challenges arise, they can refer to the book and discover techniques to employ as new coping strategies. When students have come to the end of your course, suggest that they do another textbook reconnaissance. They may find helpful materials on a second read of the content that they didn't realize would be useful to them initially. For example, Planning is an early chapter in the textbook, and it is important for setting the stage for success. If students were reluctant to try out the Time Monitor/Time Plan in the beginning of the course, now that they have a semester under their belts, they may be more likely to fully comprehend the value.

## Strategies for grading this course

**Start with an A**—Tell students they begin the term with an A and then tell them what they can do to keep it. This often is a more successful approach than telling students that they start off the course with a "clean slate" and have them work up to the A. Starting with an A is a positive motivator for students.

**Keep it simple**—Keep your grading system simple. If you don't plan to grade all of the work, define the requirements for successful completion of the course.

**Get students involved**—Have students hand in a written evaluation of their own performance, giving themselves a grade based on the course requirements.

**Devise a point system**—Assign points to regularly scheduled activities, optional or flexible activities, and extra credit activities. Give students a grid to use for tracking points early in the class. This might help students stay on track and be less anxious about grades. A points-based grading system also helps teach students an important lesson that many students new to college do not realize—a grade in a college course is created by the student. An example of a point system is available on your HM Class Prep CD.

## First day of class activities

Listed here are suggestions for warm-up activities that you can use on the first day of class. Creating a sense of community in your classroom starts during your first class meeting. Here are a few simple icebreakers to help you and your students acclimate to the classroom and the course objectives. Others are designed to help student begin work on the text itself. Additional activities are available on the HM ClassPrep CD.

**What do you want?** The new Power Process, *Discover what you want*, helps student to answer the question *What do you want?* Research indicates that more than 60 percent of first-year college and university students are not yet sure of their career choice, even if they have declared a major area of study. A student may choose a major because of parental pressure or the institution's policy rather than because of a passionate commitment to that filed of study or career. This lack of clarity about a

38

student's destination could negatively affect the student's level of dedication and involvement. The example in the new Power Process will help your students understand the important of discovering what they want and stating these goals specifically. By discussing this with your students at the beginning of your course, your students will be on their way to setting goals and learning how to create plans to achieve them. If your students are having trouble getting started answering the question *What do you want*, consider guiding them by asking them what they hope to accomplish in this course, in the term, and in the academic year. A free video entitled *What do you want* is also available to you to help your students get motivated at the start of your course. Contact your sales representative or your College Survival consultant to order this videotape.

**Introducing the text** (Contributed by Lee Jones, University of Mississippi) On the first day of class, Lee introduces his students to the text. He instructs them to go through pages one through five and count the number of times that they find the word action or some derivative. When they have written down a number, they can go through pages six through nine looking for the number of times that the word *truth* or *truthfulness* is used. The only other direction is that they should do this as quickly as possible.

Lee points out that repetition is one of the most effective ways to learn and that once a concept is stored in memory, it is available for use at any time. He asks students to consider the particular words they were searching for in the beginning of the book. He stresses the importance of action in their lives in general and in their education in particular. He emphasizes that they will get the most from their education if they participate actively in the classroom. Lee also reminds students that truthfulness and integrity are vital components of success that they can practice consciously throughout their college careers.

This exercise introduces students to essential concepts in the Student Success course. It is also a good way to familiarize students with the text and literally get them to be in touch with the pages. Consider selecting specific key words that you feel are important to your audience. For example, if you are teaching a course of student athletes, you might ask your students to find all of the examples that relate to athletes and action. Be creative! Getting your students involved is easier when you're involved!

**"Nametag" Exercise** The purpose of this exercise is to assist students in getting to know each other. They might also learn something about themselves.

**Procedures**—Distribute stick pins and 3x5 (or larger) cards, and give the following instructions (draw an example card on the board as the students fill out their cards):

1.  Write your name—first, middle initial, and last—in the middle of the card.

2.  In the upper-left corner, write three things you are good at.

3.  In the upper-right corner, name a place you would like to visit.

4.  In the lower-left corner, write three things you want to achieve in college.

5.  In the lower-right corner, list two things you like to do.

    Variations on this exercise are endless. For example, you could list two things you are proud of, two favorite foods, the most influential person in your life, a material possession you would like to own, three words you would use to describe yourself, three qualities you look for in a friend, a peak experience in your life, and so on.

6. Pin the card to your shirt, blouse, or jacket.

7. Stand up and for the next few minutes (three to eight minutes, depending on the number of people in the class) walk around the room looking at as many cards as possible. Don't forget to look at people's faces before and after you read their cards. You must do this without talking. This is the hardest part of this exercise and potentially the most educational. Notice how you want to talk. (You will probably have to remind students to stay silent.)

8. Now get into groups of three, again without talking and preferably with people you do not know. When you are in a group of three, sit down anywhere.

9. When everyone is seated in a group, have the members of each group agree on which person is A, which is B, and which is C.

10. The A's will begin. For one minute, A will tell B and C something about himself and what he has written on his card. This doesn't have to be something extremely personal, just whatever he feels comfortable relating.

11. A's minute is up. Now, it is B's turn to do the same.

12. And now C will tell the group something about himself.

13. Before you return to your seats, cover your name tags and tell the other people in your group their names. If you have forgotten someone's name, guess.

**Closure**—When students have returned to their seats, ask each student to write a Discovery Statement on his nametag and turn it in to you. The Discovery Statements will be about students' reactions to the exercise and what they learned as a result of participating. The name tags can be your means of taking attendance for the class, and you will also have an opportunity to learn something about each student in your classroom.

**Alternative**—Distribute the 5x7 cards, and skip the stickpins. Have the students fill out the cards in the same way, then have them pair up and choose to be either A's or B's. First, have the A's explain their cards for one minute; then have the B's do the same. Then go around the class and ask students to introduce, by name, the student with whom they were paired. Have them tell the class something about that student.

**Important**—At the end of all exercises during which students meet each other, have them repeat the names of the others in their group before returning to their seats. The more people a student knows, the more comfortable he becomes.

**College Survival kit: A creative thinking exercise** This exercise has been adapted from *The Creative Training Techniques Newsletter* (Minneapolis, MN) by Shirley Wileman Conrad, Ogalala Lakota College, Kyle, SD. This exercise is useful as a way to introduce the course and to demonstrate collaborative learning and creative and critical thinking.

First, put students into small "home" groups. Give each group a bag of items (eraser, rubber band, mint, etc.), with each bag having the same contents. Each group member reaches in and selects an item. Then, the groups split up, and students find others who are holding the same item. Instruct the

40

new groups to brainstorm and generate a list of how the item represents being successful in college. You can give an example or two to help students get started. After everyone has had a chance to speak in these groups, students go back to their home groups to share their discoveries. This is also a good springboard for discussion with the class as a whole about discovering what items had particular significance for students and what was surprising to them.

### The College Survival Kit

**Mint**—to remind us that we're worth a mint and that we can significantly contribute to the world around us

**Eraser**—to remind us that mistakes are unavoidable and that we have the opportunity to erase a mistake by learning from it

**Marker**—to remind us to make our mark as leaders and to create colorful, meaningful encounters

**Circle**—to remind us that we are all connected in the circle of life and that the choices we make travel around

**Magnifying glass**—to remind us to look closely at the choices that lie before us and to choose wisely

**Rubber band**—to remind us that we won't hurt ourselves if we stretch a little and that we need to know where our breaking point is

**Compass**—to remind us that there is always help to get us back on track

**Map**—to remind us that a well-laid plan will help us get to where we want to go

**Rainbow ribbon**—to remind us that we do not have to do this alone. There are others who are there to help us along the road.

**Clown nose**—to remind us that laughter is the best medicine and can see us through a myriad of situations

**Mirror**—to remind us that every job is a self-portrait of the person who did it

**Gold medal**—to remind us that attending school is like preparing for the Olympics. It takes practice, diligence, a good coach, self-motivation, and a clear picture of the goal to get the gold.

**Mastering New Stuff** Trying new techniques, changing habits, and practicing new behaviors can be uncomfortable at first. However, these activities make up much of what a Student Success course is about. When describing the benefits of a course, it is wise to be honest about the challenges as well as confident in students' abilities to be successful. Here are some techniques for making this point. Ask students to write their names with their nondominant hands, to introduce themselves to one another and to shake hands with their left hands, or to cross their arms in the opposite way from what they normally do. With practice, any of these uncomfortable activities will begin to feel natural.

**Co-creating a Syllabus** To give students an opportunity to take responsibility for what they will learn in the course, involve them in creating the syllabus.

**Step 1**—Ask students to complete the Discovery Wheel.

**Step 2**—Distribute an outline of what you are planning to cover during the term. Ask students to compare the outline with the table of contents in the book, keeping in mind the discoveries they made while completing the Discovery Wheel.

**Step 3**—Ask students to tell you what they would suggest adding to, deleting from, or changing in your outline. Also ask them to prioritize the material and tell you what they feel is absolutely essential to cover.

**Step 4**—Make any changes in your outline that you feel are appropriate, and inform students about them.

**Who Do You Think I Am?** This exercise is about our pictures of other people. While it is geared toward the students' pictures of you, the questions could be rewritten to get perceptions of anyone.

Generally, when we meet someone, we make up a story about who this person is based on how he looks, acts, talks, and so on. Our stories, formed very quickly, are built on assumptions, and any resemblance to reality is strictly coincidental. To demonstrate this, distribute an anonymous questionnaire early in the term with questions about yourself such as these:

What is my age?
Where was I born? Where did I grow up?
Am I married? Do I have children? How many?
What kind of car do I drive?
Would I get along with your friends? Why or why not?
Would you get along with my friends? Why or why not?
Will I be strict in grading you? Why or why not?
Do I support or oppose equal pay for equal work?
Did I vote in the last national election? For whom did I vote for president?
Am I a religious person?

What kinds of activities do I enjoy? Circle all that you think apply.

| | | | |
|---|---|---|---|
| scuba diving | water-skiing | golf | cleaning house |
| baking | writing | tennis | reading |
| downhill skiing | basketball | sewing | travel |

Summarize and report the results to the class and share the truth. Be prepared for a few laughs when you compare the students' pictures of you with your own pictures of yourself.

## Techniques for teaching large groups

Student Success courses often work best when the group is 25-30 students. This may not be a reality on larger campuses. Dividing students into smaller workgroups is an easy way to handle a larger group, and assigning different exercises to different groups is one way to make grading a little less tiresome. Here are some other tips.

### Learning and remembering names
- Use name tags.

42

- Promise to learn students' names—this demonstrates memory techniques as well as the effectiveness of making a promise.
- Use name tents.
- Take photos and place them on oversized cards with pertinent information. (One way to do this is by collecting student ID cards and copying them. Bring a digital camera to class or see if you can get a student to volunteer to bring theirs.)
- Request that students always state their names first before asking or answering a question or making a comment.
- Create a seating chart before the first class.
- If you miss a student's name in class, take that student out for coffee.
- Be willing to look foolish.

**Bringing a sense of community to your classroom**
- Remember students' comments and refer back to them by making references to the students' names.
- Assign students small group roles—leader, recorder, timekeeper, reporter, logistics specialist, or social director.
- Ask students to come in for individual 15-minute appointments during the first or second week of class.
- Set ground rules and consistently enforce them.

**Encouraging participation in large classes**
- Practice enthusiasm.
- Plan participation activities.
- Call on students rather than waiting for them to volunteer.
- Use a question box.
- Get students to participate: Have them write first. Then have them share in groups (two to four students).
- Read anonymously submitted Discovery and Intention Statements.
- Plan variety: Use a seven-part course structure. Lecture less.

**Handling Paperwork**
- Use a travel folder—each student should have one with in/out files.
- Color-code chapters and file folders for students.
- Lay out papers alphabetically and then have students pick up their own papers.
- Use a logistics person in small groups to pick up and deliver the group's papers.
- Use three-part quiz sheets so you don't have to hand back or correct quizzes.
- Ask your students to e-mail you assignments and then return the comments via e-mail, creating a "paperless" classroom.
- Pick up and hand out papers according to seating charts.
- E-mail students the handouts and have them print them before class.
- Use a course management system (like Blackboard or WebCT).

**Logistics**
- Use a microphone whenever possible.
- Claim the territory: Wander around. Be willing to be larger than life, even theatrical at times. Think big about gestures and movements.
- Use student assistants to help teach content, reinforce ideas, or grade papers.

- Have the students present on different topics, providing them with practice in public speaking skills.
- Videotape guest speakers.
- Vary your voice level (even speaking softly at times).

**Taking Attendance**
- Use 3X5 cards and have students turn them in at the start of class with their name and the date on the card.
- Have students sign in.
- Use quizzes, Discovery and Intention Statements, or assignments turned in as a means of taking attendance.

## Setting the stage for success: Using the Discovery Wheel

The Discovery Wheel is an opportunity for students to think about the kind of student they are and the kind of student they want to become. This exercise is assigned at the outset of the course to help students assess their current strengths and weaknesses in different areas of student success. Students answer a series of questions and then plot their scores on their Discovery Wheel—a graphic illustration of their skill levels—where each section corresponds to the chapters in the text. This exercise is also available for students to complete on the *Master Student* Web site (http://masterstudent.college.hmco.com). This is an easy way to begin to integrate technology into your classroom. Have your students print out their Discovery Wheel and bring it to class.

At the end of textbook is an identical Discovery Wheel. By repeating the exercise at the completion of the course, students can trace their progress in acquiring skills and techniques that can ensure their success in school and later in life. This upfront assessment also provides students with a high-level preview of the course content.

Remember, the purpose of this exercise is to give students the opportunity to change their behavior. Retaking the Discovery Wheel allows students to see what behaviors they have changed on their journey to becoming a master student.

Having your students complete the Journal Entry that follows this second Discovery Wheel provides them with another opportunity to state *how* they intend to change. When your students complete the Discover Wheel at the end of the text, encourage them to consider tools that they did not think they could use the first time they encountered them in the text.

**Note:** Student scores might be lower on the second Discovery Wheel. That's OK. Lower scores might result from increased self-awareness and honesty, valuable assets in themselves.

Dean Mancina, Faculty Advisor for *Becoming a Master Student, Eleventh Edition,* shares his experiences using the Discovery Wheel with his students at Golden West College:

Most of my students have not yet purchased the text when they come to the first class meeting of my student success course. I know some students are still shopping for courses and are not fully convinced that this class is going to be useful to them. So I like to take a portion of the first class meeting to sell them on the course and the textbook.

I hold up the book and show them the Discovery Wheel, explaining that this is an example of one of the useful exercises in the book. I point out that in this course, the textbook drives the class, and that it is absolutely essential to complete all of the reading assignments and related exercises before coming to each class meeting. I also use the PowerPoint slides for Chapter One to show students the Discovery Wheel in detail.

As I do so, I say, "This picture illustrates the author's philosophy of student success. There are some topics, such as planning and tests, that one would expect to be part of a study skills course. But in the holistic approach that this course takes, we see that health, diversity, technology, and many other topics are all given equal importance in achieving student success, as reflected by the sections of the pie being of equal size. When you complete this exercise, you will see, visually, your relative strengths and weaknesses in the 12 areas of student success identified by this book.

"Each chapter focuses on one of these 12 areas. At the end of the term, when you have completed the course, you'll see that one of the last exercises in the book is the post-Discovery Wheel. By completing this exercise and comparing it to your first Discovery Wheel, you'll have a picture of the progress you've made in this course. Of course, this can only happen if you do the first Discovery Wheel *now*. Make a commitment to get the book and do the exercises and assigned readings, especially the Discovery Wheel, so you'll be able to fully use the feedback you'll get at the end of this course."

The Discovery Wheel can be used in a variety of ways. Here are some additional options:

- Ask students to list their intentions or commitments for improving particular skills during the term. At the end of the term, they can assess those areas again after they complete the Discovery Wheel in the last chapter.
- Create an assignment requiring students to contact people on campus or in the community who could asst them in enhancing particular skills. For example, the reading center could provide specific strategies for improving comprehension, word attack skills, and concentration.
- Allow Discovery Wheel results to help shape course content. Students could turn in their results so you can use them to plan future lesson, or they could tell you what they want to learn or accomplish during the course as a result of their self-assessments.
- Ask students to form small groups and "coach" each other. Coaching course include how to capitalize on and share their talents and how to strengthen their areas for growth. FI you choose to do this, let students know your reasons for forming small groups. For man, their self-assessment is personal, so sharing the results might be risky. You can put students into small groups based on just one section of the Discovery Wheel. For example, pair students who feel that they have technology savvy with those students who feel that they need further assistance.
- Ask students to "coach" themselves. They can image that the self-assessment is for someone special whose success in school and life is important to them. Ask students to take their best suggestions and implement them.
- Create a resource network. Use the titles of each section of the Discovery Wheel and list one title per piece of paper. Ask students who scored high on a particular section to sign their names to that piece of paper if they are willing to assist others in enhancing their skills in this area. Then distribute the lists to the class (or post on your course web site).

## Teaching learning styles in your classroom

The *Master Student* text introduces several approaches to learning styles: the Learning Style Inventory, multiple intelligences, and the VAK (visual, auditory, and kinesthetic) system. That's a lot of information to absorb. It is important to recognize that each approach presents a valid option and is not the final word on learning styles. Encourage your students to look for ideas from any of these methods that they can put to immediate use. When they write Intention Statements, have your students keep these questions in mind: How can I use this idea to *be* more successful in school? What will I *do* differently as a result of reading about learning styles? If I develop new learning styles, what skill will I *have* that I don't have now?

## The Learning Style Inventory (LSI)

People are fascinated by why they do what they do—and students are no exception. Taking the Learning Style Inventory (LSI) in Chapter One gives students a chance to increase their self-awareness as learners. The LSI helps students make sense of what they're experiencing in college.

Developed by Dr. David Kolb at Case Western Reserve University in Cleveland, Ohio, the LSI measures a learner's preferences for *perceiving* information (taking it in) and *processing* information (making sense of what they take in). When these preferences are plotted on two continuums, four unique modes of learning are formed. Students find that while every individual is capable of employing all four modes, each person has a "preferred" way of learning.

A new feature, the Master Student Map, highlights these four modes to help students become more effective learners through an understanding of their own learning style preferences. More importantly, the Master Student Map can help increase students' effectiveness by encouraging them to use those modes that they have previously underutilized. At the end of each chapter, students can apply all four modes to the chapter's topic by cycling through the questions in the Learning Styles Application. Information on how to administer the LSI follows this section in the Course Manual, and is further supported by materials available on the HM ClassPrep CD.

## Multiple intelligences

Howard Gardner of Harvard University believes that no single measure of intelligence can tell us how smart we are. Instead, Gardner identifies many types of intelligence, described in the *Master Student* article *Claim your multiple intelligences.* By applying Gardner's concepts, students can explore additional methods for achieving success in school, work, and relationships. When students begin to acknowledge and trust all of their intelligences, they can understand and appreciate themselves more.

*Master Student* is designed to help students develop these different intelligences. New charts accompany the definitions of Gardner's multiple intelligences in the text, highlighting the characteristics of each intelligence, the learning strategies that are preferred by people with this type of intelligence, and the careers that might interest them. Have your students apply this information to their core courses. For example, a student with musical/rhythmic intelligence could write songs using lyrics based on class notes and could experiment with various kinds of background music while studying.

## The VAK system

The VAK system is a simple and powerful technique that focuses on perception through three sense channels: seeing, or *visual* learning; hearing, or *auditory* learning; and movement, or *kinesthetic* learning. Invite your students to discover their VAK preferences by taking the informal inventory included in the text.

Strategies in the text highlight ways students can build on their current learning preferences and develop new options by utilizing their other sense channels.

## Administering the Learning Style Inventory

The Learning Style Inventory (LSI) is an important tool to help your students discover their preferred mode of learning. Yet many instructors have found that students can feel overwhelmed when they are left on their own to take the LSI, score it, and interpret the results. Consider the following suggestions.

Begin by introducing the LSI to your students. The article "Learning styles: Discovering how you learn" will help you set the stage. Be sure to review with your students the step-by-step directions for completing the LSI, which begins on LSI-1. The Learning Style Inventory is printed on special carbonless paper that allows students to score their own inventories. Be sure your students remove the sheets that separate page LSI-2 and LSI-3 *before* they complete the inventory. This sheet is in place to prevent the carbonless paper from picking up stray marks students make in their text prior to completing the inventory.

The new design for the inventory will make filling out the answers easier for your students. If you are assigning the LSI as homework, consider walking students through the scoring process in class first. Or ask them to hold off scoring the inventory until they're in class with you. Refer to page LSI-2 to help your students interpret their results. Guide them in using the interpretive material—help your students connect it with their own experience. Doing so will pay big dividends. Not only will your students begin to understand why they make the choices they do, but they'll be better partners in the learning process.

Be sure to review the Cycle of Learning with your students. These three new examples will be easily identifiable to all of your students and will encourage them to put the information they have discovered about themselves into practice right away. Begin your discussion by asking students about their preferred way to learn historical information or new technology. Once you have your students in the proper mindset to think about their learning style, they will be better prepared to read the Master Student Map at the beginning of each chapter and will understand the value of completing the Learning Styles Application at the end of each chapter.

The article "Using your learning style profile to succeed in school" will have your students participating in a Mode 4 activity. Put It to Work and Career Applications features at the end of the chapter will have your students thinking specifically about learning styles and their application in the workplace.

Students can use their understanding of learning styles to make choices that support their academic progress. Ask them to consider these questions:

> **Why** should I involve myself in this learning situation?
> **What** will I need to do in order to understand the concept?"
> **How** is this learning meaningful to me?
> **What if** I apply this strategy to my other courses or to my life?

Integrating knowledge of learning styles into the curriculum can help teachers design a course that promotes success for all students. As we choose our teaching methods to address various preferences at different points in the course, we meet different students' needs. Students in our classes typically represent all four modes of learning, so some students will sometimes find a good fit with what we're doing, while at other times they'll need to stretch beyond their preferences. Acknowledging different learning styles allows teachers to shift their energy from lecturing to facilitating. Rather than just focusing on the transfer of knowledge, we use feedback about our students' learning to inform our teaching. Students come to realize that their interactions shape what happens in the classroom, and they become active participants in constructing their learning experience. Working together, teachers and students create an environment that promotes success.

As you teach, your students will be more aware of how you're involving them in various parts of the learning cycle. And they'll learn to work with you—when what you're doing matches their learning preferences, and also when you ask them to stretch.

Information regarding using the Learning Style preferences as you develop your lesson plans appears earlier in this Course Manual. After you read through this section, consider re-reading the information about lesson plans.

## Background information regarding the Learning Style Inventory

Developed by Dr. David Kolb at Case Western Reserve University in Cleveland, Ohio, the LSI measures a learner's preferences for perceiving information (taking it in) and processing it (making sense of the information). When these preferences are plotted on two continuums, four unique styles or modes of learning are formed. Students find that while every individual is capable of employing all four styles or modes, each person has a "preferred" way of learning.

**Perceiving**
In considering how students perceive information, Kolb uses a continuum ranging from **concrete experience (CE)** to **abstract conceptualization (AC)**. Those who favor perception through concrete experience generally prefer to deal with situations in a very personal way. They perceive by sensing and feeling, often taking an intuitive approach to problems. They usually function well in unstructured situations.

Those who favor perception through abstract conceptualization generally prefer to think things through. They analyze, intellectualize, and construct abstract theories to understand their experiences. They take a scientific approach to problems and often function well in clearly defined, structured situations.

For example, a teacher conducts a "get acquainted" exercise, asking students to walk around the room to introduce themselves and interview other students. Those who lean toward concrete experience are likely to be very comfortable with random mingling. Students who lean toward abstract conceptualization are more likely to prefer a set of well-defined instructions, including a specific set of questions to ask when interviewing other students. They might be uncomfortable during this exercise.

**Processing**
In considering how students process information, Kolb uses a continuum ranging from **active experimentation (AE)** to **reflective observation (RO)**. Those who favor processing new information through active experimentation generally prefer to jump in and start doing things. They immediately look for practical applications of what they have learned. They generally do not mind taking risks and are results oriented.

Those who favor processing information through reflective observation usually prefer to watch and ponder what is going on. They are generally interested in understanding a situation through careful observation. They are often capable of seeing several different points of view and can generate many ideas about how something happens. They are more likely to value patience and sound judgment.

In the "get acquainted" exercise previously mentioned, the students leaning toward active experimentation would begin immediately. They might value meeting as many people as possible and

48

will generally leave a lasting impression on those they meet. Those who lean toward reflective observation might be slow to begin and are more likely to reflect on the meaning of the exercise and to form opinions about its utility.

## Visualizing Learning Styles

Kolb depicts the relationship between how we perceive and how we process information by illustrating the processes on intersecting continuums. Refer to pages LSI-7 and LSI-8 as you read this section so that you can *see* these parts in action. The vertical perception continuum ranges from **concrete experience (CE)** on the top to **abstract conceptualization (AC)** on the bottom. The horizontal processing continuum ranges from **active experimentation (AE)** on the left to **reflective observation (RO)** on the right.

When the continuums are overlaid, unique styles or "modes" of learning are formed:
- Mode 1 (Why?)
- Mode 2 (What?)
- Mode 3 (How?)
- Mode 4 (What if?)

The labeling of the quadrants is useful only to help identify kinds of awareness. *No one mode or style is any better or more effective than another.* Individuals will generally have a preference for a particular mode, given the learning situations and environmental factors they encounter. Additionally, it is important to remember that every individual is a combination of all four styles. Following is a brief description of each quadrant.

Mode 1 (Why?) learners combine the learning processes of concrete experience and reflective observation. People with this learning style are best at viewing concrete situations from many different points of view. Their approach to situations is to observe rather than to take action. Those with this learning style might enjoy situations that call for generating a wide range of ideas, as in brainstorming sessions. These learners probably have broad cultural interests and like to gather information. The imaginative ability and sensitivity to feelings characteristic of this mode are needed for effectiveness in arts, entertainment, and service careers.

Mode 2 (What?) learners combine the learning processes of abstract conceptualization and reflective observation. People with this learning style are best at understanding a wide range of information and putting it into concise, logical form. Those with this learning style are probably less focused on people and more interested in abstract ideas and concepts. Generally, people with this learning style find it more important that a theory have logical soundness than practical value. This learning style is important for effectiveness in information and science careers.

Mode 3 (How?) learners combine the learning processes of abstract conceptualization and active experimentation. People with this learning style are best at finding practical uses for ideas and theories. Those with this learning style have problems and make decisions based on finding solutions to questions or problems. These learners would rather deal with technical tasks and problems than with social and interpersonal issues. These learning skills are important for effectiveness in specialist and technology careers.

Mode 4 (What if?) learners combine the learning processes of concrete experience and active experimentation. People with this learning style have the ability to learn primarily from hands-on experience. Those with this learning style probably enjoy carrying out plans and involving themselves in new and challenging experiences. Their tendency might be to act on "gut" feelings rather than on logical analysis. In solving problems, they might rely more heavily on people for information than on their own technical analysis. This learning style is important for effectiveness in action-oriented careers such as marketing or sales.

## The importance of understanding your learning style

The ability to learn is the most important skill a person can possess. We are continually confronted with new experiences or learning situations in life, in our careers, and on the job. In order to be an effective learner, we have to shift from getting involved (CE), to listening (RO), to creating an idea (AC), to making decisions (AE). As an adult, you have probably become better at some of these learning skills than others. You tend to rely on some skills and steps in the learning process more than on others. As a result, you have developed a learning style.

Understanding your own learning style helps you become aware of your strengths in some aspects of the learning cycle, and you can help your students do the same. One way you can improve your learning effectiveness is to use those strengths when you are called upon to learn. More importantly, you can increase your effectiveness as a learner by improving your use of the steps you underutilize.

The chart on page LSI-8 identifies the characteristics of each learning style and includes suggestions for further improvement. *Balancing your preferences* is a tool that students can use this chart to begin developing new ways to feel more comfortable in the different modes.

## Improving Learning and Problem-Solving Skills

Students can improve their ability to learn and solve problems in three ways:

1.      Develop learning and work relationships with people whose learning strengths and weaknesses are the opposite of theirs.

2.      Improve the fit between their learning style strengths and the kinds of learning and problem-solving experiences they face.

3.      Practice and develop learning skills in their areas of weaknesses.

**First strategy**—Develop supportive relationships. This is the easiest way to improve learning skills. It is important to recognize one's own learning style strengths and build on them. At the same time, it is important to value other people's different learning styles. Also, students should not assume that they have to solve problems alone. Learning power is increased by working with others. Although students might be drawn to people who have similar learning skills, they'll learn more and experience the learning cycle more fully with friends and coworkers who have opposite learning skills.

How? If someone has an abstract learning style, such as Mode 3, he can learn to communicate ideas more effectively by associating with those who are more concrete and people oriented, such as learners who prefer Mode 1. A person with a more reflective style can benefit from observing the risk taking and active experimentation of people who are more active, such as learners who prefer Mode 4.

**Second strategy**—Improve the match or fit between a student's learning style and his life situation. This is a more difficult way to achieve better learning performance and life satisfaction.

How? There are a number of ways to do this. For some people, this might mean a change of career or job to enter a new field where they feel more comfortable with the values and skills required of them. Most people, however, can improve the match between their learning style and their tasks by reorganizing their priorities and activities. They can concentrate on those tasks and activities that lie in their areas of learning strength and rely on other people's help in areas of learning weakness.

**Third strategy**—Become a flexible learner. Students can do this by strengthening the learning skills in which they are weak. This strategy is the most challenging and is also the most rewarding. By becoming flexible, students will be able to cope with problems of all kinds, and they will be more adaptable in changing situations. Because this strategy is more difficult, it involves more time and tolerance for mistakes and failures.

How? First, develop a long-term plan. Look for improvements and payoffs over months and years, rather than right now. Next, look for safe opportunities to practice new skills. Find situations that can test new skills and will not punish you for failure. Lastly, reward yourself. Becoming a flexible learner is hard work.

## Learning style modalities: addressing visual, auditory, and kinesthetic learners

Kolb's model is one of many different ways to approach learning styles. It is important to be aware of the wide variety of factors that influence a particular learning style preference. These include modes of perception or modalities (visual, auditory, and kinesthetic) and environmental factors (room lighting, temperature, sound, and time of day). The following are tips adapted from the philosophy of neuro-linguistic programming (NLP) for using modalities (auditory, visual, or kinesthetic) in the classroom.

| Auditory learners are often... | Visual learners are often... |
|---|---|
| Natural listeners | Fast-talking |
| Speak more slowly than visual learners do | Impatient |
| Speak in a monotone | Often interrupt |
| Favorite expressions: | Favorite expressions: |
| "I hear that." | "I can picture that." |
| "That rings a bell." | "It appears that . . ." |
| "Well informed." | "It's not yet clear." |
| "To tell the truth." | "We see eye to eye on that." |
| Quote other people: "He said . . ." | |
| | *Visual learners learn by:* |
| *Auditory learners learn by:* | Seeing and imaging |
| Listening and verbalizing | Using colors |
| Using songs or rhythms | Using images, shapes, drawings, paintings |
| Oral directions | Sculpting in the classroom |
| Rhymes | |
| Listening in the classroom | *Teaching strategy:* |
| | "Show" them things. |
| *Teaching strategy:* | Paint mental pictures. |
| Take your time. | Use references and examples. |
| Pay attention to sounding good. | Make reports and charts look good. |
| Plan and deliver an organized conversation. | |

**Kinesthetic learners are often...**
Slowest talkers of all
Slow to make decisions
Favorite expressions:
"I've got a feel for it."
"I grasp your point."
"It boils down to . . . "
"Sensitive."
"Motivate."

*Kinesthetic learners learn by:*
Doing and manipulating
Using body movements, dance, gesturing
Physical actions in the classroom

*Teaching strategy:*
Walk them through everything.
They will need a hands-on demonstration.
Engage their emotions.

# Embracing diversity

Research indicates that while successful students benefit from having a relationship with a caring and competent adult, they are most likely to excel if they receive positive support from a peer group. The information here will help you foster that sense of belonging and assist students of all backgrounds in sharing with each other their discoveries and insights about higher education.

Teachers and students are currently using *Master Student* in the United States, Canada, and many other countries. However, a variety of cultural and life experiences will most likely be represented by the students in your class. They will come from many places with varied experiences.

Additional activities on the HM ClassPrep CD-ROM offer ways to encourage communication among students of different races, ethnicity, ages, countries of origin, and levels of familiarity with the American language and American customs.

The video *Embracing Diversity* highlights a group of students representing diverse cultures, ages, races, and religious and ethnic backgrounds. They share their personal experiences and illustrate by example effective means of communicating across cultures. Attitudes, stereotypes, and biases are examined.

One of the major goals of diversity awareness is to understand how each person fits into the lives and world of others. For some of your students, college might be their first experience with someone different from themselves. Keep in mind as you prepare for your course that some kinds of diversity can be less obvious, though just as profound, as others. To the student from rural America, a classmate from New York or Chicago might seem nearly as strange as one from Finland or Zimbabwe, and vice versa.

52

International students will have additional adjustment issues beyond those of the other students in your class. They are far from home in an unfamiliar culture. Keep in mind that some statements, activities, or attitudes that seem perfectly natural in our society might seem curious or even offensive to students from other countries. Familiarize yourself with cultural differences and issues that could baffle or frustrate these students and work to overcome them before they become obstacles to learning.

Finding common ground can be an important learning experience in the classroom. Routinely pairing students from different backgrounds and circumstances when assigning group projects and activities can provide students with the opportunity to encounter ideas, attitudes, and experiences different from their own. Throughout the semester, schedule activities or exercises that accentuate the similarities among your students and also celebrate the differences.

## School strategies

**Promote participation**—Involving students in school activities challenges them and stimulates their interest. Promote the benefits of participating by placing "ads" in school newsletters and putting notes on bulletin boards. Design and display posters. Ask other teachers to announce school activities in their classrooms. Brainstorm ways to get more students involved. Don't overlook asking students for their ideas!

**Provide tutors**—Encourage students to take advantage of tutors. Maintaining or improving one's performance level and gaining confidence in academic ability help ensure student success.

**Structure opportunities for friendships**—Having friends is widely accepted as a critical component of making a healthy adjustment to college life and achieving academic success. Friendships can be expanded beyond immediate peer groups to include faculty members, administrative staff, counselors, role models, peers from home environments, community members, or graduate students. Organize icebreakers and get-acquainted exercises during orientation and at other school happenings. Encourage the use of name tags at these events. Sponsor social activities that include faculty and staff as well as students. Encourage broad participation in all social, academic, cultural, and extracurricular events.

**Examine policies and procedures**—Review policies and procedures, looking for any subtle (or blatant) messages of racism or other forms of discrimination. If there is no clear disciplinary procedure for infractions of any policy, implement one.

**Promote resources**—New students who are unfamiliar with the resources at your school won't use them. Asking the administrators and staff who are responsible for these resources to describe their services during student orientation is only the beginning of what's possible.

Ask administrators and directors of service programs to speak in your class. Suggest that clubs and organizations offering services to diverse students sponsor programs to familiarize students with the resources at your school. Write articles about resources for the school newsletter. An open house at which refreshments are served will encourage students to get to know the facilities and the services that are available. Ask students who have benefited from the resources to give testimonials. Create contests and games that require students to visit various offices, facilities, and services personnel.

Promote the resources at your school in such a way that they attract and serve students. Have tutors and counselors introduce themselves and make short presentations in class. Ask the student advisory board for help.

**Make school inviting**—Students who feel comfortable are more likely to experience success in school. Do the residence halls offer quiet places to study? Are exercise facilities available at convenient times? Are the needs for student transportation and day care facilities met? Are computers and software programs up-to-date? How long do students have to wait for assistance in the financial aid and other student services offices? What is the quality of the food service? How can registration procedures be more efficient? Do instructors post office hours and keep them? What do admissions representatives say would attract more students?

**Hire from different backgrounds**—Whenever possible, hiring both men and women from a variety of backgrounds will provide role models for students. Whether they are faculty, staff, or administrators, they should be knowledgeable about diversity issues and committed to being involved with students on campus.

**Evaluate faculty**—Conduct regular student and peer evaluations of all instructors. Include the criteria of being sensitive to the needs of students and being responsive to the learning styles of all students.

**Encourage leadership**—Students from diverse backgrounds who are in leadership positions help promote acceptance and inclusion of all students in all areas of school life. Sponsor leadership training programs. Encourage students with leadership potential to consider running for student offices.

**Sponsor panel discussions**—Invite students from a variety of populations to participate in panel discussions on a wide range of topics. Each panel member can introduce himself (including a description of what it's like to be a member of his particular population on your campus, if appropriate) and then state his point of view about the topic. The discussion can then be opened for questions and answers.

**Conduct workshops**—Invite faculty and staff to attend workshops on the diverse backgrounds, circumstances, and cultural differences of students at your institution.

## Classroom strategies

**Help ensure success**—You can individualize your instruction and structure your course so that students experience success. Total success in school is achieved by taking a series of small, successful steps. Set high and realistic expectations. If your course is too easy, students will lose interest. If it is too difficult, students might become discouraged. By continually evaluating students, monitoring their progress, and getting feedback from them, you can plan your classes in ways that help ensure student success.

**Provide opportunities to talk**—Invite students to speak about their perspectives. Suggest that students talk to others to share their concerns, celebrations, compliments, and complaints. Use small group discussions and exercises. Promote the idea of visiting with counselors and forming peer support groups. The suggestions for conversations and sharing on the HM ClassPrep CD-ROM include many ideas for stimulating discussions.

**Acknowledge and appreciate cultural differences**—We can learn from each other and from exploring values that are different from our own. When we exchange ideas, we can expand our perceptions and examine our values. Use conversations and sharing seeds, publications, and special events to recognize and celebrate diversity.

**Communicate the advantages of being bicultural**—Learning new ways of speaking and behaving does not mean denying or letting go of our traditional languages or customs. Adding alternatives does not eliminate anything. Expanding our options increases our ability to operate effectively in a variety of situations and improves our chances of success.

Discuss how the school environment is similar to, and different from, students' home environments. Then discuss ways to make effective transitions back and forth from one to the other. Explore how the expectations of one environment can be assets or liabilities in another. Recognize that a strength in one culture might be a disadvantage in another. Tennis rackets are great on a tennis court, but they don't work very well in a game of golf. How can a student adapt so as to be successful in both environments?

Recognize different beliefs regarding time, competitiveness, and respect for authority. In some cultures, punctuality is a plus. In others, time is not measured in hours, minutes, and seconds; instead, it is measured by the movement of the sun, the changing of the seasons, and an intuitive sense of community readiness. In some cultures, competitiveness is a common incentive toward achievement. In others, it is considered antisocial and insulting. Eye contact during conversations is considered respectful in some cultures and disrespectful in others.

You can acknowledge a wide range of beliefs and, at the same time, communicate the expectations of your institution. An advantage to being bicultural is the ability to adopt behaviors that promote success in a specific environment.

**Encourage exposure to different backgrounds**—Encourage students to break out of old patterns and habits by associating with people from different backgrounds, as well as with those whose backgrounds are similar to their own. They could choose new lab partners, form groups with people they don't know for in-class exercises, sit in new areas in the student union, or attend events that are likely to draw crowds different from those with whom they are comfortable. Invite your class to brainstorm ways to gain exposure to people with different backgrounds.

**Survey student needs**—Evaluate frequently. When you become aware that a student is struggling in a certain area, make an appointment with that student to formulate an action plan.

**Individualize feedback**—Students appreciate getting specific feedback about their individual performance. Write relevant comments on papers you return. Send messages and comments to students through the school mail. Thank a student who has actively participated as he leaves the classroom.
**Set clear expectations**—Communicate expectations clearly. State them several times in several different ways. Use examples to illustrate both what is acceptable and what isn't. Invite students to ask questions in class or to contact you during your office hours if they have any questions or concerns.

**Be a mediator**—As an instructor of a student success course, you can facilitate communication between students and administrators. Pass students' complaints and compliments on to the people who are most directly involved. Ask for responses from those people and report back to the students. Follow up on all communications until the matter is resolved.

**Include other cultural experiences**—Use speakers, textbooks, classroom materials, activities, and media presentations that incorporate diverse cultural experiences. Ask students, colleagues, administrators, and community members for recommendations.

**Use a critical thinking approach**—Ask students to decide what they think about relevant issues and why they think it. Then ask them to seek other views and gather evidence to support the various viewpoints. Discuss which view or views are the most reasonable. When discussing issues, you can apply the strategies outlined in the articles on critical thinking in the text to recognize any errors in thinking.

**Encourage proaction**—When students face uncomfortable, unfamiliar, and difficult situations, they sometimes choose avoidance. They might feel powerless or resentful and choose to withdraw rather than risk embarrassment. Help students consider the long-term costs of giving up. Help them see the benefits of a positive, healthy, and proactive approach. Suggest a variety of alternatives for dealing with the problems they face. Rather than giving up, students can garner support and find or create forums to discuss and resolve their issues.

**Allow personal expression**—Invite students to translate material into their own words. Ask them how certain techniques, or variations of those techniques, might be applied in their own culture.

**Acknowledge student expertise**—Ask students to communicate course content from their unique cultural perspective. Experiencing a concept from a different cultural perspective reinforces it. Give an assignment requiring students to combine a student success strategy with some cultural event, personality, tradition, or value. For example, they could create original music and lyrics or describe what role a particular success strategy might have played in how a cultural hero changed history.

**Use guest speakers**—Invite guest speakers to your class who represent successful role models. Ask them to share struggles they have experienced and successes they have achieved. Be sure to include time for a question-and-answer period.

## Personal strategies

**Avoid generalizations**—All generalizations are suspect—even this one. Avoid tendencies to lump together all people of one race or culture. Consider speaking up when you hear generalizations being made.

**Examine your own prejudices**—If you have painful memories that contribute to your prejudices, judgments, and generalizations, examine them. Tell the truth about the costs and benefits of holding on to them. Look at how your history encouraged you to be prejudiced in certain ways. Talk about your prejudices and formulate a plan to heal and grow.

**Examine your assumptions about students**—Where do you imagine that your students go during their vacations? How would you expect them to spend extra money? What type of music do they enjoy? Who are their heroes? Which holidays do they celebrate? Listen for how often your assumptions direct your teaching and your conversations with students. How would your teaching and your conversations be different if you assumed nothing about your students?

**Find a translator**—Taking a First Step by admitting that we are unfamiliar or uncomfortable with students from other cultures helps us bridge the gap. Ask around to find someone who can act as a translator. In this sense, a translator is someone from the students' ethnic or cultural background who has successfully adapted to the mainstream environment. Ask students if they are willing to have this person present when you discuss various issues.

**Increase your sensitivity to society's exclusions and inclusions**—When we become aware of what to look for, we can see many examples of how one cultural or ethnic group excludes or includes others. Watch advertising and television shows. Listen to speeches. Examine the policies and notice the membership demographics of schools, business organizations, neighborhoods, religious institutions, athletic clubs, and social groups. Look for blatant, formal structures as well as subtle or hidden messages of exclusion and inclusion.

**Reach out to students**—Be sure students know your office hours. Send written invitations to each student in your class to come visit you during those hours. Talk in class about what students might gain if they schedule an appointment to see you or if they just drop in. Write your reactions to what students have written on papers before you return them. Maintain accurate records about attendance and call students when they miss a class. Use whatever appropriate methods you can think of to let individual students know that you are personally interested in their success. Be a person with whom students can form a supportive, interpersonal relationship.

**Give specific feedback**—Feedback promotes student success. Be especially sensitive to the unspoken expectations of the environment at your school and in your community. When feedback is given with a sincere desire to promote success, it is likely to be appreciated.

## Racially and ethnically diverse students

The Census Bureau of the U.S. government projected in 2000 that the U.S. population will increase from 281,421,986 to 404 million in 2050. By 2100 the total population will have doubled to 560 million. While these numbers are interesting, possibly daunting, by themselves, perhaps the most telling statistics concern the racial and ethnic changes that are happening now and will continue to happen. The non-Hispanic white population, for example, will drop from approximately 72 percent today to 53 percent in 2050.

Important and exciting changes are already visible in classrooms across the United States; still, many populations do not yet feel entirely comfortable in academic settings. There is much that instructors can do to change this situation, from simply being aware of it to using specific strategies in the classroom.

As the contents of this section of the Course Manual indicate, there are many diversities represented in colleges today, and it is a constant challenge for students, instructors, and institutions to meet the needs of a diverse population. In classrooms, this can be difficult because of prevalent stereotypes, lack of familiarity with others' lifestyles, and the sheer difficulty of conducting and participating in discussions about diversity.

One starting place is to understand what "ethnicity" means. Denotatively, the term "ethnic" refers to people who share a distinct race, nationality, religion, cultural heritage, or language. Connotatively, the term might be used with less precision as in the statement, "I enjoy ethnic food." An ethnicity is something that is specific, not general, and all individuals sharing an ethnicity are unique. This is why stereotypes are inappropriate, hurtful, and untrue. We can never say that everyone from a certain ethnic background is the same.

Similarly, we can never say that all members of the same race share exactly the same characteristics. Again, stereotypes are inappropriate. The term "race" might be perceived as falling under the umbrella of ethnicity; however, in its most general or vague sense, it is understood as a term describing a group of characteristics passed on by genetics. While skin color is certainly an example, this is overly simplistic. The term "race" can bring up strong emotions, and it should not be used carelessly.

In the best of all worlds, we would not have to think about ethnic and racial diversity. We would notice similarities rather than differences, and all people would consider themselves on exactly the same plane. This is not yet true in classrooms or other places. What can instructors do to foster a comfortable, respectful environment in their diverse classrooms? How can all students be given an equal opportunity to succeed?

A number of successful strategies have been tried by many instructors in their classrooms.

**Incorporate racial and ethnic diversity in your curriculum**—Provide readings and research paper ideas about racially and ethnically diverse topics. Encourage everyone in the class, not just the racially and ethnically diverse students, to pursue these topics.

**Invite alumni as guest speakers**—Local alumni from your school are often pleased to speak to students and to answer their questions. Make sure your guest speakers represent all of the races and ethnicities in your classroom, if possible. Having them visit and speak throughout the term or semester will help foster an environment in which all people are respected.

**Encourage discussions about diversity using great care**—Discussing racial and ethnic diversity might make your students uncomfortable. Don't force the issue. However, when you cover the Diversity chapter in *Becoming a Master Student*, there will very likely be occasions when your students will want to talk about diversity. This is positive in that these discussions can lead to an open environment in which it is not difficult to broach difficult topics. However, it is very important not to let such discussions devolve into stereotypical and biased remarks, as can happen under the pretense of good humor.

Jokes, stereotypes, and biases should be addressed in the classroom, if doing so will not cause discomfort to a minority student. Speak to the student or students who make these remarks outside of class, too. See this as an opportunity for critical learning, rather than a reprimand. Help the students understand why stereotypes are inaccurate. Guide them to explore the ways that racism can emerge from an "us and them" mentality. Ask what the point of such a mentality is. If you have a student who continues to make inappropriate remarks in class, consider referring him to a counselor. This is important for the other students in your course and also for the student, who might be setting himself up for difficulty in the workplace and the broader society.

**Treat minority students as individuals**—Always treat your students as individuals rather than as representatives of a group. Never ask a student to answer a question or speak on behalf of his racial or ethnic group. No individual can speak for others in his "group." There is as much diversity within groups as there is among individuals. Do not look to your diverse students to validate a fact. When discussing issues pertaining to racism, people who don't experience such occurrences often make the person who does encounter them feel uncomfortable.

## High School Graduates

*Contributed by Ivan Favila and Mary Fleming-Hughes, Counselors, Minority Engineering Recruitment and Retention Program, College of Engineering, University of Illinois at Chicago*

When starting a Student Success course, you might want to clear up misconceptions or misunderstandings with your students as they make the transition from high school to college.

| **High School** | **College** |
| --- | --- |
| Highly structured | More flexibility |
| Dependence | Independence |
| Courses less demanding (requires less time and energy) | Courses more demanding (requires more time and energy) |
| Student is considered a child, and his parents are | Student is considered an adult, and he is held |

58

| **High School** | **College** |
| --- | --- |
| held responsible for his actions. | responsible for his own actions |
| Grades are given to parents, who have access to student's records. | Grades are mailed directly to student. |
| Student remains in classes for one year. | Student remains in classes for one term. |
| Four marking periods | One grade reflects entire semester. |
| Grades might reflect effort, quizzes, attendance, conduct, homework, and teacher's opinion of student. | Grades reflect performance on exams and projects. |
| Teacher calls parents for conference. | Professor has no interaction with parents. |
| Teacher seeks out student to offer assistance. | Student must seek out professors for assistance. |
| Student has daily interaction with teachers and parents | Student has little or no interaction with teachers and parents. |
| Counselor meets with student and parents. | Counselor meets with student. |
| Daily lectures/classroom activities | Lectures are held two or three times a week. |
| Student does not apply for financial aid | Student must apply for financial aid to be considered for scholarships, grants, or loans. |
| School creates social and cultural activities to enhance student's education. | Student must find organizations and activities of interest. |
| Student can remain in school despite poor academic performance. | Student can be dropped from college for poor academic performance. |
| Student can be suspended for disobeying rules and regulations. | Student can be dismissed from college permanently for disregarding rules and regulations. |

## The high school-to-college transition

*Article by Clare E. Weinstein, Professor, Educational Psychology; Karalee Johnson, Robert Malloch, Scott Ridley, and Paul Schultz, Graduate Students, Educational Psychology, University of Texas at Austin*

Reprinted with the permission of the National Institute for Staff and Organizational Development (NISOD) at the University of Texas at Austin. Innovation Abstracts. September 30, 1988, vol. 10, no. 21.

Community college instructors, developmental specialists, and educational psychologists are becoming increasingly more interested in the nature of the transition between high school and college. Most students enter post-secondary educational settings shortly after they complete their high school studies. However, some come to college years after they have graduated from high school. The educational reference points for both of these groups are often still grounded in their secondary school experiences. This experiential reference point can create problems for students because of the differences between the environments and the demands of high school and college learning settings. If we are committed to helping students to succeed academically, then it is part of our responsibility as educators to help students to make the transition successfully from high school (or from high-school-based expectations) to college.

Using questionnaires and an interview schedule, a study of the differences between secondary and post-secondary educational climates and requirements was conducted as part of the Cognitive Learning Strategies Project located at the University of Texas at Austin. Data was obtained from instructors, students, student affairs specialists, and learning assistance specialists. The results of this study have been pooled with other research findings to identify six categories of differences: (1) academic environment, (2) grading, (3) knowledge acquisition, (4) support, (5) stress, and (6) responsibility.

The following is an edited list of college characteristics highlighting some of the major differences between high school and college:

1. **The academic environment includes differences in operational, or logistical, variables.**
Instruction is mainly by lecture.
Reading assignments complement and do not necessarily duplicate lectures.
There are usually more students at college.
There are more social distractions.
Classes meet less frequently and for fewer hours per week.
There is less "busywork."
The tasks often are less structured and less concrete.
Instructors usually are not trained to teach.
Using the library effectively is more important.
Students are held responsible for what they were supposed to have learned in high school and in other courses.
Class discussions often are aimed at raising questions with no clear right or wrong answer.
There is much more emphasis on understanding clearly.

2. **The grading category includes differences in how grades are earned.**
Harder work is required for earning a grade of A or B.
The simple completion of an assignment often earns a grade of C or lower.
Many semester grades are based on only two or three test scores.
Student progress usually is not closely monitored by instructors.
Exam questions often are more difficult to predict.
There are more major writing assignments.
Essay exams are more common.

3. **The knowledge acquisition category includes differences in how students study and acquire new knowledge and expertise.**
Instructors rarely suggest ways that students can learn the material.
Effective reading comprehension skills are more important.
Taking good notes is more important.
Few visual and study aids are provided.
Identifying the main ideas is more important.
Effective communication skills are more important.
Students must independently seek additional and supplementary sources of information.
Students usually must recognize the need for and initiate requests for additional help.
Students need to monitor their own progress.
Paying attention in class is more important.
Studying is more important.

4. **The support category includes the significant differences in the amount of support that students receive.**
Relationships with family and friends change.
There is less contact with instructors.
There is less individual feedback.
Instructors sometimes are not student-centered.
There often is more academic competition.
Behavior problems are not tolerated.
The environment often is impersonal.

Students often are given little direction.

5. **The stress category includes differences in the concerns and perceived pressures that students experience.**
There is an increased workload and faster pace.
Students are more independent and are held accountable for their behavior.
It is more difficult to earn high grades.
An entire course is completed in 14 weeks or fewer.
Many students experience increased financial responsibilities.
Many students experience new and often increased social pressures.
Students are expected to know what they want from college, classes, life, and so on.

6. **The responsibility category includes the changes associated with a student's role in high school and in college.**
There are an increased number of choices and decisions to be made.
More self-evaluation and monitoring are required.
More independent reading and studying are required.
Students are more responsible for managing their own time and commitments.
Students establish and attain their own goals.
Students determine when they need help and must locate the appropriate resources.
Students are more responsible to whoever is paying for their education (including themselves!).
Interest in learning often must be generated by the student.
Motivation to succeed often must be generated by the student.

**Summary**—Using information we have gathered about the changes that occur when students make the transition from high school to college can help instructors and student affairs personnel to facilitate the process. Our experience with students in an undergraduate learning-to-learn course indicated that many of them were not aware of the different environmental and task demands that they would face in college. Helping students to become aware of these changes and of the roles that they will need to play in obtaining their education is an important goal for all of us who want to help students maximize their chances of succeeding in college.

## International and ESL Students

*Contributed by Joel Fleischer, Miami Dade Community College, Miami, FL*

Each year the number of international students studying in the United States reaches into the hundreds of thousands. Students who come to our shores as refugees or political asylum-seekers swell the ranks even more. In addition, a significant number of students who are native born speak English as a second language.

These students are challenged to learn a new language and to acquire a second culture as well. What's more, the educational system in our country might differ markedly from what international students expect. The result can be a continuous process of adjustment.

### Stages of Cultural Adjustment

This adjustment process might take months to complete. In order to understand this, think of the adjustment that you go through if you move to a different state or province in your own country. You adapt to the new environment; climate changes, variations in diet, and other subtle changes affect the way you act and think. This adjustment is compounded for an international student. Various authors have identified this process as "culture shock" with distinct stages.

**Honeymoon stage**—This occurs at the outset when students are eager to explore their new culture. Often these students want to please, and they cooperate with you at every level. They might smile and nod in agreement with everything you say, when in fact they might not understand you at all. This characteristically leads to the second phase of cultural adjustment.

**Hostility stage**—As their frustrations with the new culture increase, students can become angry and stressed. Often they blame the new culture for this discomfort. At this stage, students often lose interest in their work, and in extreme cases, they withdraw. During this stage it is important to be as supportive as possible.

**Humor stage**—As students adjust to their new surroundings and begin to relax, they can laugh at some of their mistakes—the same mistakes that led to problems during the hostility stage. Now students have made friends and feel more connected to their new surroundings.

**"At home" stage**—Once students feel comfortable in their new host culture and at the same time still feel connected to their native culture, they are "at home." In essence, these students are "bicultural."

## Help Students Make the Initial Adjustment

It is essential for educators to recognize special needs. In particular, instructors of Student Success courses can use a variety of techniques to help students adapt effectively. The following techniques can assist you, no matter how many international students are enrolled in your course.

**Smile**—A smile is recognized universally and can help a student feel at ease with you.

**Speak more slowly, not more loudly**—Many people have a tendency to speak loudly to a person who does not understand English. The person can hear you; he just needs you to speak slowly and clearly.

**Learn names**—Take time to learn students' names along with the correct pronunciations. Students will appreciate your effort. They, too, are working to learn new pronunciations.

**Recognize students**—Acknowledging individuals fosters inclusion and a feeling of belonging. Remember that, at first, international students will know few people.

**Show interest in differences**—Ask international students about their families and native countries. They consider this information important and often enjoy sharing it.

**Break information down**—Instead of delivering information and ideas in large chunks, experiment with explaining them step by step. Writing down key information can also help.

**Prompt for complete information**—When filling out forms, international students might inadvertently leave out information. They might not fully understand what needs to go in writing.

**Discuss faculty-student relationships**—International students can often benefit from talking about their relationships with instructors. Keep in mind that many of these students come from highly formal systems of education and family upbringing. The relatively informal relationship between faculty members and students in your school might come as a surprise. For example, many international students are not used to taking part in class discussions or even raising questions. They might be used to a system in which the teacher's word is final and not open for discussion.

62

**Interpret body language accurately**—Some Native American students, for instance, show respect for adults by avoiding eye contact. Sometimes people misinterpret this as exactly the opposite—lack of respect or interest. Instructors can learn to decode such nonverbal behavior and adapt to different styles. Talking about these issues in class can lead to new understanding for the rest of the class as well as for the instructor.

## Adapt the Curriculum

The previous suggestions are useful for the initial phases of adjusting to a new culture. Beyond this, it is important for educators to adapt traditional teaching methods. After all, those who teach English as a Second Language (ESL) impart language instruction and also expose students to our wider value system and societal norms. This calls for a flexible approach.

Certain values that international students learn at home can differ radically from what they encounter in our schools. Southeast Asian parents often teach their children that the interests of the family are primary; the individual's interests come second. Completing a class assignment can take a back seat to caring for siblings so that parents can work. This is just one example of the cultural differences, as well as the linguistic challenges, that many international students confront. Such facts call for changes in our curriculum and practices. Several suggested strategies based on concepts from *Becoming a Master Student* follow.

**Take a First Step**—International students often need an orientation to their new environment. The Student Success course is an ideal time to "tell the truth" about what they'll discover. Begin with the physical environment. Guided and self-guided tours are one way to help your students learn the locations of buildings and services. Also make time to review the structure of our higher education system. International students might not understand the differences between a technical, two-year school and a four-year university. How degree programs are organized, the concept of a liberal education, the importance attached to grades—all of these might be unfamiliar ideas as well.

Add to this the language of higher education—words such as "semester," "term," "academic advisor," "dropping a course," "freshman," "sophomore," and "major." And don't forget slang: "bombing a test," "flunking out," "cutting class," "jock course," "Greek," "prof," and so on.

**Tune in to a new sense of time**—North Americans tend to value promptness and time management. However, in other cultures the concept of time has a different meaning and level of importance. Temporal orientations vary across cultures. Some societies focus on the present (Latin America); others look to the past (China).

North American culture is oriented to the future. The value placed on deferred gratification is an illustration: "If I work hard now, I will reap the rewards of future success." Those who do not share this value might be seen as lazy.

Talking about all of this with students can shed new light on the host culture and foster respect for other orientations. It can also help instructors understand why the motivation they seek to instill in students might not "take" with people who have a different outlook on the future.

**Choose test items carefully**—Test taking is an area in which many international students find it crucial to make adjustments. Objective tests—multiple choice, true/false—have been a mainstay in North America. In contrast, international students might be more versed in subjective examinations such as essay and oral tests. Students who are used to rote memorizing and accepting the instructor's word might flounder when it comes to analyzing or synthesizing material.

What's more, students come from cultures with different literacy traditions. Some cultures emphasize oral tradition, a practice that transmits knowledge through memorizing the spoken word. Compare this to the literacy style favored by North Americans, in which students are asked to recall material based on understanding the written word.

**Take another look at "cheating"**—To many international students, cooperation and mutual help are the norm. They might not understand the notions of competitiveness or cheating. Explaining the definitions of honesty and codes of honor can lead to a fascinating discussion. Many Middle Eastern students are used to working in a co-op fashion.

Even a simple demonstration can show how we make assumptions in the absence of the facts. Take an opaque coffee mug and place a fork inside it so that only the tip of the fork is visible. Show this to students and ask them to describe what you are holding. Most will say, "A mug with a spoon." Imagine their surprise when you pull out the fork. This is a concrete way to introduce the topic of assumptions and stereotyping.

**Recognize different standards of health and hygiene**—These are two dimensions in which cultures differ widely. Both are important to discuss with international students.

One concern for many of them is health care. International students might be amazed at the cost of medical treatment in the United States and might fail to understand the necessity of securing health coverage. This is often the case for students who come from a country with "socialized" medicine.

Personal hygiene is another area to explore. You can explain this issue neutrally from the North American point of view. For example: "Americans are very conscious of smells. We frequently launder our clothes and believe in using deodorants, perfumes, and colognes to mask natural body odor." This approach differs from asking a student to bathe regularly to get rid of an offending odor. Ask students to scan magazines and to notice the number of products designed for hygiene.

**Be sensitive to how students manage personal problems**—In Western cultures, people seek help from the "outside," such as the services of a professional counselor. In other cultures, this is unthinkable. People from these cultures do not give up their personal locus of control. They quietly handle crises in the context of the family, particularly in cases involving rape, theft, emotional distress, and alcohol or other drug abuse. It might help your students to talk about this difference. Also remember that international students might be missing their traditional family support system.

**Point out resources**—Exposing international students to campus and community resources is critical. These students might not be familiar with using the library or support services such as academic advising. They might be used to taking required courses rather than choosing electives.

Stress management is a key issue. Explain how students can access counseling both on and off campus. As they go through cultural adjustment, international students might need peer support groups and an understanding ear.

Often international students rely on public transportation. Many will appreciate having route maps and related information.

### Enrich Experience Outside the Classroom
Most of the strategies suggested thus far take place in the classroom. Experiences outside the classroom can enhance cross-cultural understanding as well.

**Introduce the neighborhood**—Neighborhood tours and field trips are a place to start. By exposing students to the wider community, you help them understand the diversity of its people. Visit areas with contrasting racial, ethnic, and religious ties. Stage cultural "treasure hunts" that force interaction between students and local people. ("When you visit this Cuban neighborhood, ask about the common ingredients of their meals.") Take students to a museum so they can get a perspective on local history. See the local government in action as well. Whenever possible, use public transportation and ask guest speakers to give a miniorientation before your group departs.

**Promote volunteerism**—To underscore the value of volunteering, arrange for students to work in soup kitchens, hospitals, nursing homes, homeless shelters, or for similar organizations.

**Promote mentor and tutoring programs**—If at all possible, recruit tutors or mentors who can work with students in their first language.

**Practice flexibility and ask for feedback**—The suggestions in this section offer a start in bridging the gaps of language and culture. Beyond these, use a variety of teaching styles. Ask for feedback from students to make sure you are meeting their needs. In so doing, you go a long way in assisting their cultural adaptation.

## Returning adults

Historically, our educational systems have been geared to lecture. Although the content taught in higher education differs from the content taught to younger students, most of the models of teaching and learning used are fundamentally the same. As the percentage of older students returning to school increases, more and more educators are learning to adapt their teaching to meet the needs of these students. Often, the strategies that successfully involve older students can enhance the learning of traditional-age students as well. This section contains ideas and techniques that have proved useful for all students, particularly returning adults.

**Be sensitive to concerns outside of school**—Returning adults are often managing full and challenging lives in addition to attending school. Jobs, children, and spouses require time and energy that can interfere with educational commitments. Discuss childcare facilities, car-pooling information, and other resources that are available. Encourage students to form support groups to share ideas about particular problems. Organize study groups during the first week of class. Teach time-management skills. Ask students to discuss how the people in their lives can be part of a team that promotes their success.

**Stress practical benefits**—Older students in particular are interested in how they will be able to use what they learn at college in real-life situations. Students will be far more interested in a theory if they learn practical applications along with it. They will generally care more about answering the question "How can I use this?" than the question "Which theorist developed that idea?"

Point out the relevance of what you are teaching to life outside the classroom. Ask students to think about how they are going to put what they are learning to work in their lives. In discussions and on quizzes, ask application questions as well as literal and comprehension questions. Take field trips. Use problem-solving activities and actual case studies. Expand laboratory programs. Review your curriculum and eliminate courses that are outdated and material that is irrelevant.

**Affirm experience**—Older students generally have a greater abundance and wider variety of life experiences than younger students. Ask them for examples to illustrate a point. Encourage them to talk about, and even teach, what they already know.

Many adult learners minimize what they already know. They might be overly concerned about their deficiencies and how much they have to learn and relearn. These students might not realize the value of what they have already experienced. Acknowledge and respect the fact that they have a great deal to contribute to the classroom.

Allow students to express their anxiety about returning to school. Opportunities to air concerns can relieve insecurity and fear about this new experience. They can also serve to create an awareness that many other new students have similar emotions.

**Beware of experience**—Older students have had more time to solidify their values, belief systems, and expectations. They might resist experimenting with new strategies and accepting new ideas. Look for exercises that offer students opportunities to examine their biases, question their assumptions, and clarify their values. Have group discussions that explore new ways of thinking about things. Invite students to be open to accepting alternative points of view.

Suggest that students temporarily put aside what they "know" and approach an unfamiliar idea with the question "What if that were true?" This approach might bring new ideas to light. New ideas are built on previous ones. Potentially damaging ideas that are examined with an open, accepting, and inquisitive attitude will not harm us and will wither away naturally. Beneficial breakthroughs are born out of forgetting what we "know." Use brainstorming to help students see that there are many more possibilities in the world than the ones they can think of by themselves.

Discuss the advantages of not finding "the" answer to a question. Putting aside answers in order to remain engaged in an inquiry often leads to acceptable alternatives and innovative directions.

**Integrate students**—Returning adults have a tendency to form groups with other returning adults. This is a problem only if it is done all of the time. During exercises, devise ways to form groups that contain a variety of students. All students benefit from interacting with people who have different experiences and values and with others of different cultures, ages, and genders.

**Use guest speakers**—Invite guest speakers who completed their education as returning adults and who are involved in areas that students find interesting. Ask students for suggestions about which guest speakers they think would be beneficial. Alumni from your course and from your school make especially credible models. Ask guest speakers to relate their current careers (and lives) to their educational experience.

**Reinforce self-responsibility**—The previous education experience of most returning students was teacher dependent. Students were told what to do, when to do it, and also precisely how to do it. Some adult learners bring this passive attitude with them when they return to school. We can be careful not to reinforce that attitude. As students become increasingly more responsible for their education, they become more involved and committed. Ask them to write their educational goals, share them with the class, and relate what they do in their daily routines to achieve those goals. They are likely to discover others who have similar goals. Invite students to participate fully in class through exercises, conversations and sharing, and writing Discovery and Intention Statements. You can also give students responsibility for evaluating their own performance.

**Use contracts**—Students can design their own education in ways that best meet their individual needs and current circumstances. By using learning contracts, students are less likely to feel victimized and are more likely to be proactive. They can make choices about what outcomes they desire, which tasks they will complete to achieve a particular grade, how they will participate, what resources they will use, and how they will be evaluated.

**Have flexible scheduling**—Nontraditional students appreciate being able to take a course in the evening or on weekends. If they are in school part-time, it is frustrating for them to have to wait an entire year before a course that they need or want is offered again. Find out what course schedules make the most sense.

**Encourage outside support**—Invite partners, children, and others who play significant roles in students' lives to visit the campus. Design programs that help them feel comfortable and show them ways that they can support the students' efforts.

## Gay and Lesbian Students

Gay and lesbian students have unique needs and concerns and might face greater challenges in college than their heterosexual peers. Although research suggests that more than 10 percent of the population is gay or lesbian, this population is often not visible and thus might be underserved on campus. Instructors should be aware of on- and off-campus resources for gays and lesbians and ready to offer institutional support for them. This article discusses some specific concerns of gay and lesbian students and suggests resources that instructors can offer.

**Coming Out**—"Coming out" is a process of achieving self-acceptance in a world that is largely ignorant about gays and lesbians and often hostile to them. Gay and lesbian students come out to themselves, first, when they accept their sexuality. They might also choose to come out to friends and family, and to the campus community by discussing their sexual orientation with teachers, in papers, or in classroom discussions. By coming out, homosexual students discover that they are not alone. Coming out is a courageous act and should always be treated with respect. Instructors can make coming out less difficult for students by encouraging a climate of tolerance and support, and by discussing gay and lesbian issues in class.

**Marginalization**—"Marginalization" is the process by which the dominant culture pushes minority cultures to the margins of society through exclusion. It is a problem for all minority groups. Even those homosexual students who have come out might feel intimidated in social settings in which heterosexuality is assumed. In class discussions, avoid "heterosexism"—the attitude that assumes that all individuals are heterosexual. Also avoid labeling individuals as straight or gay and perpetuating myths about the causes of homosexuality or supposed characteristics of gays and lesbians. Strive for inclusion of all students and for the deconstruction of stereotypes and attitudes that keep homosexuals and other minorities on the outside.

**Health**—Substance abuse, nicotine addiction, suicide, and sexually transmitted diseases are all disproportionately severe problems in the gay and lesbian community. To help prevent health problems among this population, educate your students about campus resources that are available to them, such as counseling and health centers. Many counselors and medical professionals have received training on how these issues affect gay men and lesbians, and can therefore be a valuable source of support for them.

**Finding a voice**—Direct students to the library for gay and lesbian newspapers, directories of gay and lesbian organizations, and research on gay and lesbian culture. The Web is a particularly good source of information on gay and lesbian issues and groups. Try **http://www.gay.com** for information about news, activism, relationships, health and fitness, finance, and travel. Or do a web search on "gay support" or "lesbian support."

If a gay or lesbian student believes he or she has been discriminated against, campus antidiscrimination policies and local, state, or federal laws might provide avenues of recourse. Check your institution's web site for information on its policies, and see the Gay Politics and Law site at **http://www.indiana.edu~glbtpol/** for information on laws and legal resources of interest to the general gay and lesbian community.

## Students with Disabilities

### The Americans with Disabilities Act and service to students

*We would like to thank Sharon Hinson Davis, Ed.D., R.D., L.D., for sharing her expertise and experience with us in this section. Sharon was a selected presenter at the Student Success Course Colloquium in Toronto, Canada, in 1996 at which she presented on this topic. Sharon is the assistant director of the University of Arkansas Medical Sciences/Veterans Affairs Medical Center Dietetic Internship, Little Rock, AR. She is also an assistant professor in the Department of Nutrition and Dietetics, College of Health Related Professions, University of Arkansas for Medical Sciences. Sharon has worked at the VA Medical Center in Little Rock and in education for 25 years.*

The number of students with a disability who receive a full secondary school education and who participate in a college education has increased in recent decades primarily because of (a) the passage of the Americans with Disabilities Act (ADA), which defines the rights, coverage, and eligibility requirements for citizens with disabilities; (b) the influx of older learners returning to college with accompanying disabilities; and (c) advances in medicine and technology.

The ADA (Public Law 101-336) is based on the Rehabilitation Act of 1973 (Public Law 93-112). Four definitions are essential for a clear understanding of the ADA in higher education.

Under Section Ib(3) of the ADA, a disabled person is defined as (a) an individual with a physical or mental impairment that substantially limits one or more major life activities, and (b) having a record of such an impairment or (b) being regarded as having such an impairment. "Major life activity" is interpreted as being able to care for oneself and [to] perform common tasks such as walking, seeing, hearing, speaking, breathing, learning, and working (EEOC, 1992). "A qualified individual with a disability" (Section 101[8]) has (a) the requisite skills, experience, education, and other academically related requirements for admission to a program; (b) can fulfill, with or without reasonable accommodations, the essential requirements/functions of students at each stage of his education; and (c) does not pose a direct threat of substantial harm to the health or safety of others. Finally, "essential requirements/functions" are those physical abilities, mental abilities, skills, attitudes, and behaviors that students in educational programs must evidence, demonstrate, or perform at each stage of their education (Essex-Sorlie, 1994).

The conditions presented by a student might or might not be defined as a disability based on state statutes, the courts, and previous case law. Those students with a record of the disability as a result of public school identification or of an assessment done by qualified professionals have little difficulty providing the college or university with the documentation necessary to indicate that a disability exists.

68

*The student is responsible for documenting a disability and requesting accommodations. Colleges and universities do not have a duty to inquire into the existence of a disability and are specifically prohibited from making inquiries (Milani, 1996).*

Students entering colleges or universities can acknowledge a disability, provide documentation, sign up with the disability support services, and request accommodations. The expectations of services and accommodations by these individuals (and their parents) presently exceed those of disabled students in past years. Many of these students have developed extensive coping mechanisms and deal successfully with the limitations that their disabilities have imposed. On the other hand, students might not be aware of or acknowledge a disability due to the stigma attached. These students might be known only as poor test takers or poor students. Many disabilities are not identified until the student leaves the slower pace of high school and the supportive environment of home.

Disabilities can be visible or invisible. Although research studies divide types of disabilities differently, they generally fall into one of five categories: sensory, physical, learning, behavior, and chronic health. Sensory and physical disabilities are most often thought of when disabilities are discussed. However, the number of students with learning disabilities consistently makes up 23 percent of the total number of students with disabilities and might require the most complex accommodations. Many students with physical or sensory disabilities provide their own accommodations. Their primary concern might be accessibility to the campus, classrooms, restrooms, and labs.

Students with disabilities do not have common characteristics, nor do they have the same types of disabilities. Disabilities occur without respect to age, sex, intellect, physical characteristics, race, economic status, social standing, or geographical location. Therefore, each student, even those with the same disability, will have specific and unique needs. The best way to determine the individuality of his requirements is to ask the student requesting accommodations. A frank and open discourse between the student and the instructor is the foundation of a successful education experience.

The institution is responsible for the following:

1.     A campus that is accessible to students with disabilities

2.     Development of policies and procedures that include (a) a definition of disability, (b) a statement of eligibility for services to include a medical/professional documentation of a disability, (c) a statement on confidentiality stating who should or should not be informed of the disability, and (d) a description of prohibited discriminatory actions in admissions and readmissions

3.     Providing and paying for the requested accommodation if the device is used principally to fulfill essential educational requirements and is not used throughout the student's daily activities. The institution is not obligated to provide the most expensive accommodation and is allowed to supply one that will meet the needs of the student

4.     Providing education to administrators, staff, and faculty concerning the ADA, resources available, and teaching methods specific for students with disabilities

The student is responsible for maintaining a positive attitude regarding his disability, the quality of his education, and his own learning. No one else will be able to gain knowledge or acquire skills for him. In addition, he is responsible for the following:

1.    Documenting a disability by pursuing and paying for a workup and diagnosis from a qualified professional

2.    Requesting needed accommodations in writing

3.    Requesting accommodations within an appropriate/reasonable time frame (An institution might have to purchase equipment, or an instructor might have to develop materials.)

4.    Demonstrating a willingness to negotiate on types of accommodations or materials

5.    Following college or university rules related to the use of the accommodations provided

6.    Seeking information actively, asking questions, listening, and being resourceful

## Teaching tips for the instructor

1.    Become knowledgeable about the ADA and the institution's policies and procedures on students with disabilities and confidentiality. Visit the disability support services and meet the resource people who can provide services to students with disabilities and to you as an instructor. Review the accommodations that are available in the disability support services office and in other departments such as the computer lab. Add disability support services staff to the list of guest speakers for your Student Success course. If your facility does not have a disability support services office or an individual who is responsible for those functions, visit those of a nearby college or university.

2.    Identify clearly the requirements and/or functions essential for successful completion of the class. Teaching methods that will aid all students in your class include the goals/objectives of the class, a list of assignments, examples of acceptable assignments, a method or example of evaluation for each assignment, a vocabulary list, the requirements for each grade level, and attendance requirements. Constructive feedback is vital on all assignments. There should be no surprises for the student. DO NOT ASSUME ANYTHING.

3.    When a student with a disability enrolls in your class, you might infer that the student meets the basic admission policies of the institution. While the student will have completed high school, he will have a disability and possibly also have the same problems as other entering freshmen—poor study habits, poor reading and writing skills, and so on. Do not let the disability of the student overshadow either the needs or the talents of the student.

4.    If the student does not acknowledge a disability or request accommodations in the class, the instructor is not to inquire into the existence of a disability or offer accommodations. The student must then meet the academic and attendance requirements of the class. However, during the class on how to become a master student, the student can be made aware of student and disability support services on campus.

5.    When a student with a disability requests accommodations, provide these accommodations as discreetly as possible. Even when you are accommodating students with very visible disabilities, other members of the class might feel cheated. The instructor does not owe other members of the class an explanation of the accommodations provided. However, if accommodations are instructor controlled, such as extended test-taking periods, oral exams, or requests for take-home tests, the instructor might consider extending the accommodation to all members of the class.

6.   Use a problem-solving approach to identify and implement reasonable accommodations for the student with disabilities after the obligation to accommodate has been established. The best way to determine needs is to ask the student who is requesting accommodations. Do not assume that you know what accommodations this student needs—disabilities are as individual as the students who have them. In addition, you might review the recommendations made by the specialist who evaluated the student for documentation of disabilities and check with the disability support services or an appropriate representative on campus.

7.   Accommodations generally fall into one or more of the following categories: (a) assistance by personnel, for example, a reader or interpreter; (b) technology such as a computer/laptop or assistive listening devices; (c) materials including large print or Braille materials/books; and (d) instructor-controlled activities such as extra time for test taking or schedule changes. Many accommodations can be provided at the discretion of the instructor. Provide instructor-controlled accommodations that have been requested by students in a reasonable and timely manner.

8.   Document and date the requests made by the student with a disability and the accommodations provided by the institution and/or instructor. A good-faith effort to work with the student is essential to avoid litigation.

9.   If possible, locate a faculty or staff person with a similar disability and discuss teaching methods with him or her. It is vital to use extreme caution in this situation. Always ask the student's permission before introducing him to another individual with a similar disability or setting up a mentoring program. You might also need to check with your administration for permission or advice on how to proceed.

10.   If and when the occasion arises, outline in writing the responsibilities of both the instructor and the student with disabilities and negotiate a mutually satisfying agreement.

## References

Americans with Disabilities Act of 1990 (Public Law 101-336).

Bowman, O. J., and D. K. Marzouk. "Implementing the Americans with Disabilities Act of 1990 in Higher Education." *The American Journal of Occupational Therapy* 46(6): 521–533.

Davis, Sharon H. *"The Americans with Disabilities Act: Impact on Dietetic Education."* Dissertation in partial fulfillment of the requirements for completion of the Doctorate of Education, University of Arkansas–Fayetteville, May 1994.

Henderson, C. *College Freshmen with Disabilities: A Statistical Profile.* Washington, DC: American Council on Education, HEATH Resource Center. (ERIC Document Reproduction Service No. ED 354 792).

Milani, Adam. "Disabled Students in Higher Education: Administrative and Judicial Enforcement of Disability Law." *Journal of College and University Law* 22(4): 989–1143.

Yuker, H. E. *Attitudes Toward Persons with Disabilities.* New York: Springer, 1988.

## Resources for Visually Challenged Students

College Survival and the *Becoming a Master Student* program have a commitment to the entire first-year student community. The Eleventh Edition of *Becoming a Master Student* will be available from

Recording for the Blind and Dyslexic. Please contact the Recording for the Blind and Dyslexic at 800-221-4792.

## Captioning Services

A list of companies providing captioning services is available from the Instructional Television and Media Services Department of the National Technical Institute for the Deaf. The department suggests that if you plan to have a program captioned, first define your needs and then obtain price quotes and references from at least two contractors.

To receive this list or for more information, call or write to the Instructional Television and Media Services Department, National Technical Institute for the Deaf, Rochester Institute of Technology, P.O. Box 9887, Rochester, NY 14623, 716-475-6581.

## Students with learning challenges

*Contributed by Bill Jones and Bill Racherbaumer, Monterey Peninsula College, Monterey, CA*

Over the years, the term "learning disability" has been defined in different ways by numerous government agencies, educational organizations, and school districts. Although most definitions include several common elements of learning disabilities, the label is often misunderstood and continues to generate many misconceptions. The resources given at the end of this section direct you to more information about learning disabilities.

All of us have strengths and deficiencies in the way we process information. On a continuum, some of our deficiencies interfere more with our learning than others. Most of us are able to compensate and balance our learning processes so that our deficiencies do not noticeably interfere with our ability to read, write, comprehend, solve math problems, and so on.

People with deficiencies that lead to a more severe and noticeable impact on academic performance are said to have learning disabilities. It is a matter of degree only. In other words, all of us have unique strengths, weaknesses, learning styles, and ways of processing information. The following strategies that are effective for teaching students with learning disabilities are equally effective for teaching any student.

Maintain high and realistic expectations—Establishing high and realistic expectations for students contributes to their success. This is especially true of students with learning disabilities. We are doing ourselves and students a disservice if we overreact to a disability and lower our expectations for achievement. A student with learning disabilities might require more time or need to use different strategies to be successful. Expectations of high performance standards can be maintained, and performance most certainly can be extraordinary.

Accept mistakes—Very few of us perform a skill perfectly the first time we try it. Rarely do we fully comprehend a complex concept when we first hear about it. Learning involves trial and error, practice, repetition, and mistakes. Mistakes provide feedback so that we can learn, grow, and improve. Failing or making mistakes might indicate the need for more practice, or it might suggest that we try a different strategy. Academic failure is not a reflection of personal worth.

Communicate self-responsibility—One of the most helpful decisions any student can make is to accept responsibility for creating value in his own education. Too often, having a learning disability is used as an excuse by students, parents, and educators to transfer the responsibility for learning to someone other than the student. Educational institutions and teachers are responsible for meeting the needs of students by providing appropriate educational opportunities. The responsibility for learning rests with the student.

**Use multi-sensory teaching techniques**—Say it, show it, and do it. Follow the seven-part course structure outlined in Part II of this manual. Stress the "Use your body" memory techniques described in the Memory chapter of *Becoming a Master Student*. Like all students, those with learning disabilities can learn to compensate for deficiencies by combining and balancing stronger learning processes and modalities.

**Individualize learning**—Be sensitive to the preferred perceiving and processing modalities of students. If, for example, a student needs more time to take a test, schedule special test-taking sessions or allow oral tests. Use small groups and peer tutoring. Encourage students to investigate how they learn and to give you suggestions about how best to individualize their instruction.

**Encourage candid communication**—Students can be prepared to discuss their learning disabilities with fellow students, teachers, counselors, and administrators. They can be assertive about having their needs met. They can request special testing formats, find out if there are alternatives to written assignments, arrange for teaching assistants and tutors to provide extra help, structure unique study groups, learn about services and resources that are available on campus and in the community, establish personal support networks, and educate others about the nature of their learning disability. Some students find it helpful to meet with instructors and counselors on a weekly basis, even if it is just to say hello. The more understanding that can be generated about learning disabilities, the easier it is for everyone, including the student, to promote individual success.

**Encourage planning**—Long-range academic planning and career counseling help students choose paths that are compatible with their strengths and, consequently, help ensure success.

**Suggest taking fewer class hours**—If students can accept that it will take more time than they had planned to complete their formal education, they might be able to improve their chances for success. They can take fewer classes each term and have more flexibility to balance easier classes with more difficult ones.

**Promote compensatory techniques**—Resources and strategies that can be beneficial include using tape recorders, finding a study partner in each class, forming a study group, attending all classes, asking questions in class, sitting in the front row, buying textbooks in advance, visiting instructors and classrooms prior to registration, listening to audio versions of textbooks, touring the library, and locating test files.

A group brainstorm might generate many more helpful ideas. Consult experts. You are not and should not be alone.

## Student Athletes

Athletes are unique learners, contending with the usual concerns of students, such as social commitments, challenging academic pursuits, and personal/family problems, and also with the pressures of competition, the possibility of injury, physical fatigue, and tremendous time-management challenges. Balancing academics and athletics is a challenge for student athletes in their first year of college. In addition, some (though not all) athletes arrive at their post-secondary experience under-prepared academically. Many instructors see athletes as disinterested academic observers who are protected by their coaches and the school's athletics department. Misconceptions include the following: athletes care only about sports. They are inherently not very smart. They have more muscle than brain. Athletes make it through the college or university experience on favors rather than academic effort. Gaining national sports recognition is more important to most athletes than gaining any measurable amount of knowledge or skill from the post-secondary experience. Right? Wrong!!

Athletes are often motivated, controlled, disciplined, and physically and spiritually connected individuals. Many athletes are kinesthetic learners, and as such they are easily distracted and prone to multiple stimuli overload—the result of having overactive sensory receptors. Instructors who are working with kinesthetic learners should increase the opportunity for practicing a new skill by doing, and should encourage students to stand and stretch at periodic intervals (usually every 20 minutes). If you are teaching with the seven-part course model you can easily allow for a stretch as you change activities.

Teachers often complain that their students, especially athletes, have frustratingly low attention spans. Many of us learn in 20-minute spans, with the greatest information absorption occurring at the beginning and end of each attention span peak. In other words, we pay attention at minutes one and 20 and everything in the middle is lost, to a lesser or greater degree. Learning for athletes is greatly facilitated when the instructor breaks the lecture into smaller units.

In order to better facilitate the academic success of athletes, multi-sensory, active learning strategies are recommended. Accelerated learning techniques provide some interesting and exciting alternatives for athletes. Students are encouraged to learn in high-energy environments that reward initiative and boost self-esteem. Lessons are presented with a multidimensional approach that accommodates different learning styles, speeds, and needs.

*Becoming a Master Student Athlete* is a text that is focused on the needs of student athletes by integrating examples that athletes can relate to more readily, and includes coverage of additional stressors facing student athletes. If you are teaching a course that includes student athletes, or is specific to this population, ask your College Survival consultant to send you a desk copy of this text.

**Practical Hints for Teaching Athletes**

- Let them know that it's OK not to be the "hot shot" in class.
- Make sure, though, that you make room for more reticent, introverted students to participate if they want to.
- Become the classroom coach, constantly and consistently encouraging active learning. Let your student athlete stand in class or during tutorial sessions. Walking around the room is OK, too. Don't insist, though, that every student should do this.
- Open a conversation with the athlete regarding academic attitudes and goals. You might be surprised to find out that you are the first instructor to do so.
- Discuss time management. How many hours of athletic responsibilities does the student athlete have in a week? Where can he consolidate, prune, and save energy? How can he utilize travel time to away games in order to review notes, listen to lecture tapes, and so on?
- Reinforce the Power Process "Be here now." Let your student athlete know that daydreaming is normal. Teach the student how not to get involved in a mental tug-of-war when daydreaming begins.
- Tell the athlete to attend class. Travel and practice schedules might lead to an unavoidable absence. Make videotapes of your classes available to all students who have to miss classes.

- Tell the athlete to communicate often with instructors. There is no better way to dispel the "dumb jock" myth than to personally exhibit an interest in learning.
- Use sports analogies. Recall is greatly facilitated for many athletes by image generation, especially if the subject can be related to a sports image.
- Suggest that athletes practice relaxation exercises. Conscious relaxation in the classroom can aid in controlling those constantly firing sensory receptors.
- Be flexible. At times, the student athlete might need to disregard the text organization in an effort to learn the material in an "easy-to-difficult" format. Remember that athletic training does not begin with the most difficult physical maneuver, so why should learning?
- Move around and use your hands when explaining concepts and procedures.
- Send the student athlete to the chalkboard or marker board as often as the lesson allows.
- Use basic Montessori methods when instructing student athletes.
  o Input—Monitor reception of stimuli from the environment.
  o Integration—Associate new material and make connections with what the student already knows.
  o Output—Use physical (gestures) and vocal expression of new ideas.
  o Feedback—Monitor output and adjust the system for better response.
- Finally, consider this idea. Many students report that simply knowing the time of day they were born is a great asset in trying to achieve maximum academic effectiveness. Think about it. What is the first thing that babies do after birth? They cry and then sleep. Our biological clocks are set at birth. Many students report that they experience downtime shortly after the time of day that they were born. They avoid studying during these hours as it is usually not productive. Sounds strange, and it works!

## Students at Christian-affiliated colleges

Many of the Power Processes, success strategies, and ideas discussed in *Master Student* are aligned with Christian principles. This section suggests ways to incorporate scripture into your lesson plans. A special thanks is extended to Marita Morgan of Oral Roberts University, Tulsa, OK, for contributing the scriptural examples.

Scripture can give depth and credibility to the messages in *Master Student*. The events and relationships recorded in the Bible have universal meaning. The teachings of the Bible can have significant relevance in our daily lives. Incorporating these teachings into your course can help students focus on the content. Learning can be reinforced through exposure to scriptural examples of key concepts. Students can increase their appreciation for how Christian perspectives of life can be applied to their practical goals of being successful in school.

### Make it meaningful
In some circles, *Becoming a Master Student* has been accused of promoting humanistic ideals, New Age doctrines, or Eastern mysticism. The Power Process in Chapter One in, "Ideas are tools," suggests that students should not believe any of the ideas in the book. The techniques and principles included in the text have been collected from many different sources. No doctrine or ideology is endorsed. Not even the practical techniques and strategies are endorsed. The text suggests experimenting with all of these, adopting what is effective, and putting the rest on the shelf. Students can use their own value systems as the criteria for selecting those ideas and techniques that they will use.

Just about any issue, concern, objection, or criticism can be turned into a valuable discussion that helps students clarify Christian values in their daily lives. For example, if the New Age concern arises, students can be asked to consider this question: "What are the messages of New Age ideology, and how are they similar to or in what ways do they contradict Christian principles?"

Another valuable discussion can be generated concerning the meaning of the Power Process "I create it all." Is this a prideful attitude denying that God creates all things? Or can the concept be perceived as being aligned with Joshua 24:15: "Choose you this day whom you will serve . . ."? Does it simply mean that we are responsible for all of our behaviors? Does it mean that we choose our actions and reactions, that we choose which ideas to incorporate into our lives, and, in this sense, that we "create" our experience of the world? How does having been redeemed and forgiven allow us to design, build, and respond to life differently than if we had not been redeemed and forgiven?

You can always look for different ways to use Scripture to begin conversations and sharing, to design exercises, and to create test questions. A seed for conversations and sharing, for example, could be to ask how John 8:32 is related to the Discovery Wheel: "You shall know the truth and the truth shall set you free." How does this relate to II Corinthians 5:17: "If any man is in Christ, he is a new creature, the old things passed away; behold new things have come." By discussing these passages, students can focus on the realization that being "in Christ" involves telling the truth. This First Step of self-analysis helps us see our strengths and weaknesses. The next step is to become a "new creature" through changing our habits. You could even have students rename each Power Process using a Biblical verse. Asking students to rename concepts using Biblical references helps reinforce the ideas, gives students more ownership of the concepts, and enhances their ability to articulate the principles of their faith.

Another assignment could be "Discuss the memory techniques that are illustrated when Peter remembered the words Jesus had spoken: 'Before the rooster crows, you will disown me three times.'" The answer could include talking about the memory techniques "Make it meaningful," "Create associations," "Remember something else," and "Combine memory techniques" from the text.

### Scriptural Connections to the Text
Scripture related to material in *Master Student* can be used as seeds for conversations and sharing. Assignments can include researching and writing about Biblical quotes that connect the ideas and techniques in the text to Christian teachings. Ask how one particular Scripture is aligned with several different ideas in the text. Following are a few examples that relate to various key topics:

**Goal setting**—I Corinthians 9:24–25: "Do you not know that those who run in a race all run, but only one receives the prize? Run in such a way that you might win. And everyone who competes in the games exercises self-control in all things. They then do it to receive a perishable wrath, but we are imperishable."

**Goal setting**—Jeremiah 29:11: "For I know the plans that I have for you, declares the Lord, plans for welfare and not for calamity to give you a future and a hope."

**Discovery Wheel**—II Corinthians 5:17: "If any man is in Christ, he is a new creature; the old things passed away; behold new things have come."

**Tell the truth**—Proverbs 28:13: "He who conceals his transgressions will not prosper, but he who confesses and forsakes them will find compassion."

**Discovery Statements**—Ephesians 4:25: "Laying aside falsehood, speak truth, each one of you, with his neighbor, for we are members of one another."

**Intention Statements**—Proverbs 16:3: "Commit to the Lord whatever you do, and your plans will succeed."

**Master students**—2 Timothy 2:15: "Study to show thyself approved unto God, a worker who does not need to be ashamed, rightly dividing the work of truth."

**Money**—Ephesians 4:19: "My God shall supply all your needs according to His riches in glory in Christ Jesus."

**Time management**—Ecclesiastes 3:1–8: "There is an appointed time for everything, and there is a time for every event under heaven. A time to give birth, and a time to die. A time to plant, and a time to uproot what is planted. A time to kill, and a time to heal. . . ."

**Time management**—Ephesians 5:15–17: "Be careful how you walk, not as unwise men, but as wise, making the most of your time. . . ."

**Time management**—Proverbs 16:9–10: "The mind of a man plans his way, but the Lord directs his steps."

**Goals**—Psalm 37:4: "Delight yourself in the Lord, and He will give you the desires of your heart."

**"Be here now"**—Hebrews 2:1: "We must pay more careful attention, therefore, to what we have heard so that we do not drift away."

**Memory**—John 14:26: "The helper, the Holy Spirit, whom the Father will send in My name, He will teach you all things, and bring to your remembrance all that I said to you."

**"Love your problems"**—Matthew 5:44: "But I say to you, love your enemies, bless those who curse you, do good to those who hate you, and pray for those who spitefully use you and persecute you."

**Reading**—Daniel 5:8: "All the King's wise men came in, but they could not read the inscription or make known its interpretation to the King."

**Note taking**—Isaiah 30:8–9: "Now go, write it on a tablet before them and inscribe it on a scroll, that it might serve as a witness forever. For this is a rebellious people, false sons, sons who refuse to listen to the instructions of the Lord."

**"I create it all"**—Matthew 15:11, 19: "Not what enters into the mouth defiles a man, but what proceeds out of the mouth, this defiles the man. For out of the heart come evil thoughts, murders, adulteries, fornications, thefts, false witness, slanders."

**"I create it all"**—Joshua 24:15: "Choose for yourselves this day whom you will serve. . . ."

**Study groups**—Ecclesiastes 4:9–10: "Two are better than one because they have a good return for their labor. For if either of them falls, the one will lift up his companion. But woe to the one who falls when there is not another to lift him up."

**Study groups**—I Thessalonians 5:11: "Encourage one another, and build one another up. . . ."

**Testing**—II Corinthians 13:5: "Test yourselves to see if you are in the faith: examine yourselves!"

**Testing**—James 1:5–6: "If any of you lacks wisdom, let him ask of God, who gives to all men generously and without reproach, and it will be given to him. But let him ask in faith without any doubting. . . ."

**Anxiety**—II Timothy 1:7: "For God has not given you a spirit of fear, but a spirit of love, power, and a sound mind."

**Anxiety**—I Corinthians 14:33: "For God is not a God of confusion but of peace."

**Creativity**—Isaiah 40:28–31: "God . . . the creator . . . does not become weary . . . He gives strength . . . increases power . . . those who wait for the Lord will gain new strength; they will mount up with wings like eagles, they will run and not get tired, they will walk and not become weary."

**Communication**—Hebrews 10:24: "Let us consider how to stimulate one another to love and do good deeds . . . encouraging one another."

**Relationships**—Philippians 2:3–4: "Do nothing from selfishness or empty conceit, but with humility of mind let each of you regard one another as more important than himself; do not merely look out for your own personal interests, but also for the interests of others."

**Relationships**—Matthew 5:44: "Jesus said, love your enemies, and pray for those who persecute you. . . ."

**Relationships**—Ephesians 4:32: "Be kind and compassionate to one another, forgiving each other, just as in Christ God forgave you."

**Relationships**—I Corinthians 10:24: "Let no one seek his own good, but that of his neighbor."

**Relationships**—Philippians 2:14: "Do all things without grumbling or disputing."

**Relationships**—I Corinthians 13:1–13: "Love is patient . . . kind . . . not jealous. . . . Love does not brag . . . is not arrogant . . . does not act unbecomingly . . . does not seek its own . . . is not provoked . . . does not take into account wrongs suffered, rejoices in truth, never fails." (Many of these statements can be translated into positive Intention Statements.)

**"Employ your word"**—Proverbs 10:9: "He who walks with integrity walks securely, but he who perverts his ways will become known."

**Diversity**—Matthew 37:39: "You shall love your neighbor as yourself."

**"Choose your conversations and your community"**—Ephesians 5:12: "Do not let any unwholesome talk come out of your mouths, but only what is helpful for building others up according to their needs, that it might benefit those who listen."

**"Choose your conversations and your community"**—Philippians 4:8: "Finally, brothers, whatever is true, whatever is noble, whatever is right, whatever is admirable—if anything is excellent or praise worthy—think about such things."

**Knowledge**—Ecclesiastes 12:9–10: "In addition to being a wise man, the Preacher also taught the people knowledge, and he pondered, searched out, and arranged many proverbs. The Preacher sought to find delightful words and to write words of truth correctly."

78

**Health**—I Corinthians 3:16–17: "Do you know that you are the temple of God, and that the Spirit of God dwells in you? If any man destroys the temple of God, God will destroy him, for the temple of God is holy, and that is what you are."

**Health**—Romans 12:1–2: "I urge you therefore, brethren, by the mercies of God, to present your bodies a living and holy sacrifice, acceptable to God, which is your spiritual service of worship. And do not be conformed to this world, but be transformed by the renewing of your mind, that you might prove what the will of God is, that which is good and acceptable and perfect."

**"Be it"**—Philippians 3:13–16: "Forgetting what lies behind and reaching forward to what lies ahead, I press on toward the goal for the prize of the upward call of God in Christ Jesus. Let us, therefore, as many as are perfect, have this attitude; and if in anything you have a different attitude, God will reveal that also to you; however, let us keep living by that same standard to which we have attained."

**"Be it"**—Proverbs 4:25–27: "Let your eyes look directly ahead, and let your gaze be fixed straight in front of you. Watch the path of your feet, and all your ways will be established. Do not turn to the right nor to the left; turn your foot from evil."

**"Be it"**—Proverbs 23:7: "For as he thinks within himself, so he is."

**Attitudes**—Philippians 4:6–7: "Be anxious for nothing, but in everything by prayer and supplication with thanksgiving let your requests be made known to God. And the peace of God, which surpasses all comprehension, shall guard your hearts and your minds in Christ Jesus."

**Attitudes**—Hebrews 4:12: "For the word of God is living and active and . . . able to judge the thoughts and intentions of the heart."

**Do something you can't**—Ephesians 4:13: "I can do all things through Christ who strengthens me."

(NOTE: Scriptures were taken from the New American Standard Version of the Bible and the New International Version.)

# Technology in the classroom

First-year experience courses provide students with a foundation of effective practices to utilize in higher education and beyond. It is essential that this foundation include an introduction of how to use technology successfully. "Success in the traditional classroom doesn't always translate into success when college courses require the use of online technology," starts the *E-Learning Companion: A student's guide to online success* by Ryan Watkins and Michael Corry of The George Washington University.

Increased coverage of technology topics are now included in a new chapter of *Becoming a Master Student,* Eleventh Edition and *Becoming a Master Student, Canadian Fourth Edition.* Technology is integrated into the *From Master Student to Master Employee* text, and appears as a separate chapter in *Becoming a Master Student Athlete.*

Technology promotes new forms of active participation among faculty and students, students with other students, and students with multi-media resources. While some institutions have introduced student success courses in distance learning environments, instructors have reported the highest level success by introducing hybrid course formats that integrate face-to-face course meetings and distance learning solutions.

Since students and instructors have varying levels of technology expertise and savvy, the Master Student technology resources address a wide body of resources for all levels. Access the Master Student Web Site at http://masterstudent.college.hmco.com; use the PowerPoint slides in your classroom; enroll your students in a Blackboard or WebCT course that has Master Student content already provided for you; ask your students to complete their assessment and accomplishments report using the HM Assessment and Portfolio Builder; help your students explore additional resources related to their future with the Career Resource Center. The possibilities are endless.

Here are just a few ways that instructors can use technology to enhance learning:
- Provide an electronic syllabus to each student via email or on the Web that can supply further information about assignments, expanding upon a printed version that is distributed in class.
- Electronically distribute lecture outlines, exam review questions, or study tips.
- Ask students to share their papers with the whole class via email, listserv, course management tools (like Blackboard or WebCT) or the Web.
- Assign students to respond to questions about a case study before the class discussion.
- Provide web links on the latest data that you are currently covering in class.
- Designate one of your office hours as a "virtual" office hour during which you engage the ideas and questions sent to you by students via email. This might encourage students who don't feel comfortable speaking in class or coming to your office to talk to you.
- Encourage students to participate in the discussions on the Master Student web site.
- Ask students to complete their Discovery Wheel on the Master Student web site.
- If you or your students are interested in taking or teaching a course that is online, take the assessment "E-Learning Readiness Self-Assessment." The assessment will provide you with feedback on your readiness to be successful in online courses, and help you to guide your path as you develop necessary skills and habits. If you or your students need extra assistance, consider two texts: *E-Learning Companion: A Student's Guide to Online Success* by Watkins and Corry, and *Teaching Online: A practical guide* by Ko.
- Begin your semester with the HM Assessment and Portfolio Builder by asking students to think about their skills, attitudes, values, and behaviors.

## Using the Master Student Web Site

Logging onto the Master Student Web Site (http://masterstudent.college.hmco.com) will allow you and your students to access materials related to the text you are using. This website is equipped with articles, exercises, tests, discussion groups, web resources, PowerPoint Slides, and much more, to your students better understand the concepts presented in the text and to encourage the use of these concepts in their life in and out of the classroom.

A wealth of material is presented on this website for each chapter of the text. Additional **Articles** as well as key articles from the text directly related to technology and the Internet are updated on a regular basis on the website. These articles can be assigned as part of the required reading in your class, or given as supplemental readings.

An index of **Exercises** provides both an online version of many Exercises, Practicing Critical Thinking, Journal Entry, and Discovery/Intention Statements from the text itself, as well as other activities unique to the website. Many of these activities offer a way for students to email their responses directly to their instructor. Some exercises also include a **Discussion Group** that provides the student with a forum to share their opinions and experiences with others.

An online version of the **Discovery Wheel** provides a dynamic way for students to use this wonderful assessment tool. The student will be able to view and print their completed Discovery Wheel. Follow-up questions then encourage the student to consider the implications of and their reactions to this assessment. Their responses can be emailed to their instructor.

**ACE Practice Tests** can be used as a way for students to evaluate their understanding of the strategies and concepts presented in the text. These tests are offered for every chapter to students an immediate indication of their strengths and weaknesses. Instant feedback can help students prepare for in class quizzes and tests. The ACE Practice Test questions are unique to the website and do not use questions from the test bank on the HM Class Prep CD.

**Remembering Cultural Differences** is a series of brief articles that describe a practical application of the many different facets of cultural diversity, and then ask the student to consider how these differences can hold meaning and use in their own lives. Ask you students to respond to these questions via email or in a live or web-based discussion.

A new **Master Student Hall of Fame** includes additional articles that provide a brief biography of the Master Student Profiles featured in past and previous editions of *Master Student* textbooks. This will help students garner addition insight into the importance of the accomplishments of these Master Students. Each of the biographies also includes a Internet links students can use to jump-start their own personal exploration or to perform further research for writing essays.

**PowerPoint Slides** are available on both the Instructor's and Student's website. For instructors, these slide presentations can be used to enhance classroom lectures. For students, they can help to reinforce concepts from the text, or they can be used to solidify their understanding in preparation for tests.

Additionally, the **Resource Center** provides links for the student to many other resources on the Houghton Mifflin website. Encourage students to take advantage of these academic tools for further strategies for writing, speaking, Internet use, and math skills. Information about the Houghton Mifflin Scholarship Essay contest is also available in the Resource Center.

The **Tip of the Day** pop-up feature gives the students a daily reminder of useful strategies and motivational advice from all of our Houghton Mifflin Student Success authors.

Encourage your students to submit their own **Student Voices** and reactions, opinions, and insights that they have developed in their relationship with the text. Encourage your students to use this opportunity to share their feedback with us as they reflect on their experiences with the strategies and concepts in the text. Instructor's can also share their feedback this way via our web site. Your voice will be heard, and may even appear in a future edition of the textbooks.

Much consideration and work has gone in to the creation of this website to make it a useful tool to supplement your classroom. All of the features, exercises and articles available here can be used either as an assigned portion of your class, or as an outside research and learning tool for your students to access in their own time. In either case, the tools provided on the *Master Student* website are intended to add an interactive dimension to the skills and applications that are addressed in the text.

If technology is available in your classroom, provide your students with a walk-through of the Master Student web site on the first day of class. Show them how to access the home page (http://masterstudent.college.hmco.com) and select the textbook they are using. Ask your student to bookmark this page or save it in their "Favorites" folder.

When the Internet is discussed in class, it is important to remind your students to think critically about the information posted on a web site. Anyone can post information on the Web. Have your students ask themselves questions about the source of the information, how respectable and relaiable the source is, and what evidence there is to support the information being presented. Teach your students to properly cite a web site as a source. Works appearing on the Internet should be cited along with any other outside source material. The electronic address (URL) should appear at the end of the entry.

"How do I document sources from the Web in my works-cited list?"" <u>Modern Language Association Online. 28 December 2004</u> <http://www.mla.org/style_faq4>

## Inviting students to use the Internet

- Ask students to find a web site that pertains to something that interests them in the text's table of contents on the first day of class. Invite them to submit their findings to be posted on the Master Student web site by e-mailing collegesurvival@hmco.com. Any materials sent to this e-mail address will receive confirmation (which can be used for grading).
- Ask students to visit the Web to discover more information about the Master Student Profile highlighted in the text or to search out information about their own personal heroes. Ask your students to create a "profile" of their personal Master Student.
- Ask students to visit your school's home page and conduct a scavenger hunt for resources available to them. The kinds of information that the students can search for include library hours, computer resources, academic advising, public safety tips, financial aid, professional organizations, and specific degree requirements.
- Assign students to teams of three to search the Web for additional information on material from a chapter of your *Master Student* textbook.
- Invite students to investigate the Web for unique career opportunities and transferable skills.
- Have students access one of the online Learning Style Inventories (LSIs) described in the text and then take the test and write a Discovery and Intention Statement about their results.

82

## The HM Assessment and Portfolio Builder and Career Resource Center

The HM Assessment and Portfolio Builder CD-ROM is a personal development tool that engages students in **self-assessment, critical thinking,** and **goal-setting** activities to prepare them for college and the workplace.

Students build a portfolio by responding to questions about their skills, attitudes, values, and behaviors in four key life areas: **Personal, Interpersonal, Career,** and **Community**. The **Accomplishments Report** summarizes the results of their responses, and asks students to provide supporting evidence for responses in which they rate themselves as highly proficient. This provides great practice for honing critical thinking skills as well as for creating a résumé or preparing for interviews.

The Accomplishments Report module also provides access to additional resources, such as Houghton Mifflin's Web-based Career Resource Center, which offers tips, exercises, articles, and ideas to help students succeed on their journey from college to career. **The Bridge from College to Career** lets students practice new skills acquired in college that can be applied as they enter the job market. **Finding the Perfect Job** helps students fine-tune their résumé writing and interviewing skills. And **Skills for Your Future** provides strategies for problem solving and decision making to help students learn to work with others and communicate on the job.

Each module (**Personal, Interpersonal, Career,** and **Community**) has a series of statements. Students assess their response to each statement by selecting from four choices. Feedback is provided for each response to help guide students to making the most appropriate selection. The items that students mark as *usually and consistently* true will be carried over to the **Accomplishments Report,** the fifth module.

Once the assessment portion has been completed, students will be ready to enter evidence into their **Accomplishments Report.** This is the section where students will provide supporting evidence for statements that were rated as *usually and consistently* most like their skills, attitudes, values, and behaviors. The evidence is saved and a portfolio of accomplishments is generated from these entries. Students can view and update their portfolios throughout the semester, and print a hard copy to bring to class or use for preparing for interviews.

After the **Accomplishments Report** is generated, students will see which areas still need documentation and can explore information and resources for gaining experiences in college using the **Career Resource Center**. Students can access tips, exercise, articles, and additional Internet links to help them succeed in college and in the workplace. Suggestions for using the HM Assessment and Portfolio Builder to create a résumé and prepare for interviews are also available on the **Career Resource Center**.

## Using your HM ClassPrep CD-ROM

The most powerful technology tool available to you is the HM ClassPrep CD-ROM that accompanies your *Master Student* textbook. This is an instructional resource that you can access electronically and customize to meet the needs of your course. Each resource is provided in the file format we think will be most useful to you: Microsoft Word files for documents you might want to edit, PowerPoint files for presentation, and a digitized video.

You can access the files on HM ClassPrep directly through the HM ClassPrep interface. This interface organizes resources for you by chapter or by asset type. Using the HM ClassPrep interface, you can open files in their appropriate applications, use them as they are, or modify them and save them to your hard drive. The HM ClassPrep CD works across both PC and MAC platforms.

If you wish to access files without using the HM ClassPrep interface, you can find all of the resources in this application in a folder titled Assets on the root level of your CD. The Word file contents.doc, also on the root level of your CD, provides a list of all HM ClassPrep files and their file names.

The HM ClassPrep CDs for the *Master Student* textbooks gather in one place a variety of resources to make your Student Success course easier to teach. Within an easy-to-navigate interface, HM ClassPrep gives you the following assets created specifically for *Becoming a Master Student*:

- An introduction to the CD-ROM for the instructor
- A transition guide for moving from the previous edition of the book
- Sample syllabi
- Descriptions of all components available for the Student Success course
- Exercises for each chapter
- Lecture ideas for each chapter
- A customizable test for each chapter
- A PowerPoint slide presentation for key topics
- An overview of the Learning Styles Inventory
- Video clips to help you administer the Learning Styles Inventory
- A "commercial" for the new *Power Up* Power Process video
- An index to the contents of the CD-ROM

Directions for getting your HM ClassPrep CD started on your computer are included with the disc.

The materials are organized in two ways: by asset and by chapter. To access chapter materials and assets, click a chapter number and title in the left menu, and the chapter's assets will appear on the right. Then, click an asset to launch the asset in its application, such as Microsoft Word or PowerPoint. You can now print documents, save them to your hard drive, cut and paste material from them, or edit them. After you edit documents, be sure to save them to your hard drive. (Note: Office files will be marked "Read-Only." These files can be edited. Save them to your hard drive using the Save As command on the File menu and name them accordingly.)

If you have the full PowerPoint application available on your computer, you can edit and save the PowerPoint slides included on HM ClassPrep to your hard drive or to a disk. With this feature, you can add campus-specific information to your slideshow or delete content that you feel is not relevant to your student population—and still have professional looking slides. If you do not have the full PowerPoint application, you must install the PowerPoint Viewer to play the slide presentations.

## Course management systems

Course management systems are tools educators can use to deliver instructional materials, communicate with students, and take care of record keeping, scheduling, and other instructional management tasks on computer (generally using a web browser). These systems can be used to create complete, stand-alone distance education courses or to provide supplements to traditional classroom instruction. There are two types of course management systems:

- Unique systems created by individual institutions or instructors using authoring software

- Customizable preprogrammed systems offered by commercial companies on their web sites

Houghton Mifflin Company provides you with a customizable course shell to use with the *Master Student* textbooks. Content includes Master Student Maps, Power Process Articles, and Case Studies. A facilitator's guide includes prompts for discussion groups. Ask your College Survival Consultant or your sales representative how you can get access to this resource. Prepare for your online or hybrid course by setting up materials for the semester *early*. Remember, new lesson plans and new technology take time to get accustomed to!

## *Mastering the College Experience:* A Telecourse for *Becoming a Master Student*

*Mastering the College Experience* is an integrated instructional system that combines stimulating and informative video lessons produced by the Emmy Award-winning Coast Telecourses with Houghton Mifflin's best-selling *Becoming a Master Student* text, a Telecourse Student Guide, and a Faculty Manual. The course is designed to be offered in a variety of formats, including broadcast, cablecast, or videotape delivery, all under an instructor's direction. Telecourse students study independently, watching the video lessons and reading the course-related materials on their own, at home, in a learning center, at a training site, or at the workplace.

*Mastering the College Experience* has been instructionally designed to meet the needs of students who are entering college from high school or are returning to further their education. There are 26 half-hour videotapes providing examples, methods, and resources in an engaging format. Students will be introduced to key concepts as they watch students learn and discuss the process based on discovering the power of self-responsibility. *Mastering the College Experience* features real situations experienced by real students enrolled in college. The telecourse documents the adversities and accomplishments of seven students from different ethnic and socioeconomic backgrounds as they learn core study skills as well as life skills.

A Telecourse Student Guide for *Mastering the College Experience* (published by Houghton Mifflin Company) contains overviews that summarize critical information and terms in each lesson. It serves as an important bridge between the textbook, which is required reading for participating in the course, and the video components. Lesson objectives alert students to course expectations and the information that they must acquire from each lesson in order to successfully master their own college experience. A Faculty Manual (published and distributed by Coast Learning Systems) contains information on managing the course. There are program descriptions, lesson objectives, suggestions for communicating effectively with students, a checklist of tasks for the instructor, ideas for supplementary activities, suggested techniques for providing support to students, and a list of useful references and resources. A complete test bank is also included. A Telecourse Student Guide is available for the Eleventh Edition of *Becoming a Master Student*.

# Student retention, assessment and outcomes

For nearly everybody, assessment is a part of life. In institutions of higher learning, it is a basic tenet. We assess ourselves. (Did that class session work? Is there a better way to present that material? Even a look in the mirror before leaving the house is a form of self-assessment.) We assess others. (We evaluate student performance on tests, assignments, and exercises. We give grades. We might even serve on committees that determine tenure, promotion, or compensation.) Likewise, others (the department chair or program coordinator, the dean, the students) assess us. A little intimidating, isn't it?

Assessment of the Student Success course can have at least three objectives: (1) measurement of levels of student learning, (2) evaluation of individual course sections and/or instructors, and (3) overall assessment of the Student Success course as part of a comprehensive retention program. Try viewing assessment as a means to refine your course. Many institutions use uniform assessment instruments or methods. If these do not provide you with sufficient information applicable to your Student Success course, consider employing some of the research instruments mentioned in this section to supplement your assessment process. Whether you are a new or a veteran instructor, you might find the information on assessing student learning especially helpful as you modify your course throughout the term.

This section provides a campus wide perspective on creating a welcoming and supportive experience for your students who have just arrived at college. However, a Student Success course is not likely to resolve all of the difficult issues facing your students if there are other aspects of the academic, social, or physical environments or agencies for support that need to be assessed and improved.

American College Testing indicated decades ago that in order to improve retention, a college or university campus must improve service at every point at which the student interacts with the institution. This section allows you to consider whether your campus has areas for improvement and also gives you a chance to celebrate what you are doing well.

Students often leave school when the costs outweigh the perceived benefits. As consumers, it isn't the big issues that irritate us as much as the insidious frustrations. These could be easily changed if someone on campus with a service-to-student point of view notices and brings them to the attention of the people responsible. Perhaps you are the person who will finally remedy a situation that others have found annoying and have never taken an action to resolve.

As you proceed through this section, keep in mind that the Student Success course as an isolated entity probably will not significantly increase retention rates. It will, however, enhance a comprehensive retention program. Remember that the lack of a sense of connection to the institution often contributes heavily to students' failure to continue with their studies. This sense of estrangement can be especially prevalent in the groups of students considered in this section. The nature and design of the Student Success course can foster a feeling of inclusion among students. Adding specific academic and life skills to this feeling of belonging will only strengthen your students' ability and determination to persevere.

A new pre- and post-course assessment for adopters of the Eleventh Edition of *Becoming a Master Student* was created by Laura Goppold at Central Piedmont Community College, NC. Goppold was seeking out the answers to these questions: What are my students learning? How can we find out what information these students retain? What, if anything, are they NOT learning? Find out how you can use her pre- and post-course assessment (or the model that she used) to determine what information your students are retaining in your course.

Your HM Class Prep CD has customizable evaluations you can administer to your students.

## Classroom and school strategies

Student success is a function of activities taking place at many different locations within a school and involves every teacher, administrator, and staff person. This section offers strategies for improving student retention inside and outside the classroom.

The problem of students dropping out of your college is too big to be solved merely by teaching a Student Success course. Many educators believe that presenting a course on how to be successful in school is the single most effective strategy for decreasing dropouts. And all agree that more can be done. The problem is significant.

The following suggestions come from a series of workshops presented by Dave Ellis to thousands of educators in the United States and Canada. The procedures outlined next are a condensation of his lectures. If you would like more information on any of these ideas, please call College Survival at 800-528-8323.

As suggested to students in the text, use only what works for you. Look through this list of student retention ideas. Some of the following suggestions will be senseless for your school. Many of them might already have been implemented. Check what you can implement, then devise a plan to bring it about.

**Own it all**—"But it's not my job. I know that somebody ought to do it, but that's not why I was hired. And besides, if I did try to do something about it, I would probably just make someone mad." Yes, that might be true. Change can be upsetting. The suggestion is to do what you see needs doing, even if it is not your job—even if someone might get mad. Look around, see what needs to happen to promote student success at your school, and then make it your job to see that it happens. If you "own it all," that doesn't mean you have to do it all. It just suggests that you make sure somebody does.

Look around the room in which you spend most of your work time. Look around the institution as a whole and ask yourself: What needs to be done? When you come up with several answers, pick one. Develop a plan for getting it done and then put your plan into action. Break out of the mold of tunnel vision. Walk around as if you own the place and act accordingly.

**Recognize student priorities**—Our natural tendency is to assume that students are as interested as we are in the subjects we teach. "Surely students understand and appreciate the importance of what I teach." They don't always.

Most students have priorities far different from those that educators usually recognize. Far ahead of the class material, students' priorities include grades, graduation, part-time jobs, children, money, relationships (spouses, friends, lovers), sports, purchases, and on and on. As educators, if we recognize this priority structure, it is much easier to provide relevant incentives for effective student behavior. If you want students to devote time and energy to course material, you usually have to provide a consequence for the assignment (quiz, discussion, report). Even with some of the most motivated students, it just doesn't work to say, "For tomorrow, I would like you to read all of Chapter Seven. It is not anything you will be tested on, and it is not critical to the rest of the material in this class, but it is very interesting. I'm sure you will enjoy it."

The attitude of some teachers seems to be "Well, too bad. If students are going to learn only material that they will use in the next class or sometime soon, or if they will learn only that upon which they will be tested, or if they are only interested in what is immediately relevant, too bad." Too bad for the student and for the teacher. Student priorities are not what we often wish they would be. We can either ignore the fact or we can assist students to grow by recognizing and working within their priorities.

**Provide tutoring**—A modest amount of individual assistance is often just what is needed to get a student from a position of "I'm completely lost" to "Oh, I get it now!" Tutoring can come from several sources, even when budgets are tight.

Peer tutors are often the answer. Students will usually tutor other students at a very low cost to the institution. This can be set up through a student service center, counseling department, dean's office, or the library. It is possible at most schools to offer student tutors credit (maybe just transcript credit that does not apply toward graduation) in addition to money, or even in lieu of money. High-achieving students are often sensitive to the opinions of future employers. Students recognize the credibility demonstrated when an interviewer sees a résumé or transcript showing good grades and also the ability to tutor others.

Tutoring can also be handled by full-time professional tutors or as an adjunct responsibility for faculty members. Tutoring provides an alternative to large group or traditional classroom instruction, neither of which works well for some students.

**Examine the registration process**—A common theme on college campuses seems to be "Wow, you should see our freshman registration. What a zoo! If a student can make it through that experience, he is bound to be persistent enough to graduate." There also seems to be a fatalistic attitude that implies that nothing can be done about it.

Many colleges have effectively computerized and/or decentralized the registration process and thereby removed long lines, increased student scheduling options, and humanized an often robot-like interchange between students and advisors.

Registration is often the students' first impression of your school. First impressions are lasting.

**Realize that commitment is not enough**—Educators often accuse failing students of not being motivated. Evidence seems to suggest otherwise. Students are motivated to succeed. Students generally start college by telling everyone they know. It is a big deal. They announce to friends, family members, and the guy at the corner store that they are "off to college." Students are aware of the costs. If you are not convinced of that, listen to the complaining when they pay for books or tuition. They also know the benefits of an education. (Most of them didn't enroll for the fun of going to class.) Students have a great deal invested in success.

For some students, going to school represents a last chance for breaking a failing pattern. They have high hopes as they begin their education. They are motivated. Motivation or commitment is often not enough. Flying at an altitude of 30,000 feet in a Boeing 747 can be frightening if the pilot and copilot suddenly disappear. No matter how much motivation you have, you are not likely to learn how to fly in time to safely land the plane.

To learn a complex new skill, we need to learn one small piece at a time. By blaming failure on lack of motivation, we too easily ignore a road to success—divide and conquer. Almost any student can learn

88

highly complex material if it is presented in small pieces and if mastery of each piece is gained before moving forward.

What appears to be a lack of commitment is usually an avoidance of continuing failure. Most of us quit and become "unmotivated" after repeated failure and little or no experience of success. The solution to this dilemma is to build on success. Jon Carlson, when interviewed by Bob Edwards on National Public Radio, told this story. A little girl came to him one day and said, "Dr. Carlson, Dr. Carlson, look at my paper." She then showed him a paper upon which every word was spelled wrong. He said, "Maureen, I really like your paper. The margins are nice and neat, and your printing is clean and readable." She replied, "Thank you, Dr. Carlson. I've really been working hard on it. Next I'm going to work on my spelling."

**Identify potential dropouts**—Labeling or categorizing can often lead to a self-fulfilling prophecy. It can also be a useful tool in determining where to place valuable resources.

When you identify students who are likely to drop out, you create an opportunity to promote them in ways that might not be necessary for all students. They might get special tutoring, reduced schedules, remedial classes, extra encouragement, or supplemental learning material.

Research studies proliferate on the most reliable way to predict potential dropouts. Suggestions include looking at high school grades, college entrance test scores, socioeconomic indices, and even personality characteristics. Many researchers agree that the simplest and most effective predictor of students who will drop out is first-term grades. Those students who fail one or more classes during the first term of college are most likely to drop out before completing their education.

While failure might not cause more failure, it does predict it well.

**Make counseling available**—No matter what the budgetary constraints of your institution, you can make counseling available to students. If it is not possible to have a trained and certified personal counselor at your school, you can still make one available to students. Establish a referral arrangement with a local counseling agency.

Communities of almost every size have public or church-funded counseling agencies that will set up a referral system with you. You will then have a direct and easy path for students to get help in coping with problems of divorce, death, alcoholism, children, stress, and so on. Some counseling agencies work on a sliding fee scale, so money does not have to be a barrier to getting help.

**Perform a climate check**—Often we don't know what is going on with students. It is easy to assume the best or the worst. Check it out. Find out what is going on with students at your school. You can assess student opinion formally with a written survey or informally with "Psst, hey, what do you think of this place anyway?"

**Schedule faculty hours**—A frequent complaint of students seems to be "I know I should go see the teacher, but I can never find him." When students are reminded that their teacher has office hours from 2 to 4 p.m. on Tuesday and Thursday, they often retort, "Yeah, well, I went to see him during those hours two different times, and he was never there." What the student doesn't know is that one of these times the teacher had a faculty meeting and the other time he was just down the hall getting a cup of coffee.

Students are usually reluctant to approach teachers outside of class. Once they do get up the courage to come and see a teacher, it is important that he be available. Include at least one visit with the instructor as part of the grade for this course. Consider setting aside an hour or two a week when students know that, without fail, the teacher can be easily located. The excuse "He's never around" is thereby eliminated.

Tour the school as a student. It is easy to miss seeing how your school looks through the eyes of a student. The routine of our day-to-day work can slowly blind us to the realities of our institutions. Once every week or two, put on your "student glasses" and walk around the school. Look at the buildings, look at the walls, floors, and bulletin boards as if you were a student. Read announcements from the perspective of a student. Sit in the business office or the financial aid office and wait for an appointment. Look at the faces of the people behind the desks. Ask yourself what it might look like and how it might feel to a student.

Glance in open classroom doors. Better yet, sit in a classroom for an entire class, not for just a few minutes. Imagine yourself as a student; then make a list of all that could be changed so that students would more likely be successful. Take on two or three of the items on your list as projects to accomplish. Keep a journal about your experiences and observations, and share parts of your journal in class.

**Videotape yourself as you teach**—This is one of the most effective faculty development tools around. The taping can be done by a student or a staff person from the school's media resource center. The viewing is best done privately. Supervisors can add so much additional tension to the viewing that personal insights are almost impossible.

Seeing yourself on videotape can be unsettling. Most of us are shocked the first time we hear our voices on a tape recorder. That experience is magnified when sight and sound are combined. One way to get value from the viewing is to set up a VCR, a TV, the tape of your class, and a box of tissues in a private room. Then take notes.

When viewing the videotape, be certain to record as many compliments as suggestions. Our tendency is to see with a critical eye only. Balance that with a commitment to write at least as many positive evaluations as negative ones.

**Concentrate efforts on first-term students**—Student retention research indicates that by far the largest concentration of students leaving school is during and right after the first quarter or semester. This is the most effective time in the student's career to provide additional support.

Look around to see what can be done to ensure the success of first-term students. What is needed? An extended orientation course as described in this Course Manual is certainly one way to provide extra assistance to first-term students. Improving the quality of instruction for first-term students is another option.

It is typical in colleges to assign more experienced instructors to upper-division classes. As a reward for experience and excellence, teachers are given the students who have been in college the longest. This might be a nice reward for teachers; however, from the standpoint of student success, the policy is ineffective. New students, more than any others, need the most experienced teachers. Consider having those teachers who know how best to capture student attention be the teachers who work with first-term students.

**Orient parents and spouses**—Let a student's spouse or parents know what is available at the school. Develop a short orientation program so that the significant people in students' lives can have a direct experience of the institution that is going to be demanding so much of their time, money, and energy.

This is an opportunity to "sell" the whole family, the student's primary support group, on the value of the college experience. If they are sold, they are much more likely to be supportive of the long hours and hard work required to be successful in school.

**Use alumni**—Financial contributions are all that is usually requested of past graduates. They can offer much more. Consider using them as department advisors, career consultants, or guest speakers.

As department advisors, they can meet once every few months with the head of the department, a few faculty, and other alumni to discuss proposed departmental changes, curriculum additions or modifications, placement strategies, or new directions in the field.

Alumni can act as career consultants by working through the placement department and by being willing to talk to students who are exploring career options. In addition to standard career consulting techniques, students can often gain tremendous insight by visiting with someone "in the field." This visit is even more relevant when the professional is a graduate of the school the student is attending. It is best if the student can visit the alumnus's workplace.

As guest speakers, alumni can add timeliness and credibility to almost any message or content presentation. They can certainly add variety. Most people like to teach, and alumni are often willing to donate time and energy when given a chance to share their expertise.

**Continue to "sell" students**—This idea is offensive to some administrators and many professors, who consider themselves "above that sort of thing." Selling has gotten a bad name in academic circles, and the idea of viewing students as customers is unacceptable to some. Please use another term if you prefer.

Most of us need to be continually reminded that we are spending our lives on what is important and valuable. We want to know that getting up in the morning, fighting the traffic, and spending the day working are not in vain. Students want to know the same thing. Students can be reminded of the value of their "purchase" by teachers in class and by administrators through letters and brochures. As teachers, we can interject brief messages of encouragement and support, such as "Last night when I was reading about ———, I realized again how exciting and worthwhile it is to study," or "I was pleased to find out about the job a former student is doing at such and such a company. He graduated from our department."

**Know that "not enough money" is an excuse**—While, this is not always true, generally it is the easiest answer to the question "Why are you dropping out?" We are not always aware of our motivations or the reasons behind our behavior. Maybe when a student says he is dropping out because he can't afford it, what he is really saying is "Given what I am getting, it is not worth it." At that point, it is supportive of the student's success in school to ask him what he is getting, or better still, not getting.

After the student knows you have heard his concerns about not having enough money, it is often effective to ask, "If you had enough money, why would you want to drop out?" He is likely to shake his head and state, "I didn't say I would drop out if I had the money." "Well, would you?" you can ask. "Yeah, I think so. I just failed my second accounting test, and I just think I am in the wrong major."

When the first excuse is money, the second reason is often the bottom line. If you can deal with that concern, often the problem of not having enough money can be more easily resolved. The student might do more part-time work, borrow money from someone in the family, sell something, postpone buying something, or discover a new source of financial aid.

Often, as in the previous example, the second reason has something to do with failure. Repeated failure, especially in a new environment not associated with many successes, can quickly lead to an avoidance response. When students don't experience at least some success in school, they are likely to leave.

**Reward students**—Establish rewards for just about anything you can imagine. Set up a rewards ceremony every few months and acknowledge every major and minor accomplishment possible. Pass out plaques, ribbons, certificates, and trophies. Have a special dean's list for part-time students. Award for grades, attendance, skill levels achieved, and so on. Be corny! Surely in this day of sophistication, you might argue, students are not going to accept a sophomoric display or crass reinforcement of positive behavior. Try it. We all love it.

Or don't try it. If you are convinced that students don't need or want this type of corny public acknowledgment and recognition, then skip this idea. Experiment with lots of different strategies for promoting student success and use what works.

**Hold a presidential luncheon lottery**—Identify the people on your campus whom students see as the administrative leaders. They might be the president, the chancellor, directors, and deans. Then set up a lottery in which students sign their names and phone numbers on tickets and drop them in a box. Each month, three names are drawn, and those students go to lunch with the president (or the person whom you believe students see as having the most influence at the institution). Make this luncheon a big deal. Everybody gets dressed up and goes to one of the nicest restaurants in town. The school pays.

The advantage of this type of meeting is that it lets students know that their opinions are valued. This is a time for students to talk and for the president to listen. Students can share their concerns and voice their complaints without listening to defensive justifications or worrying about having to "solve" problems. This is not a time for a "state of the university" address. It is simply a time to listen to students. Many administrators do not take the time to be with students. They slowly lose touch with what is happening in the lives of students. This is a monthly chance to find out what is needed and wanted by the people we are dedicated to serve.

**Have a "donuts with a dean" program**—Design a structure for inviting students to have donuts with a dean. Use a lottery, ask teachers to recommend students, send random invitations, or have contests. This variation of the presidential luncheon lottery allows more administrators to have more direct contact with more students. This idea can be modified to facilitate students having donuts with their teachers as well.

**Establish student internships and externships**—Provide a work experience for each student sometime before he graduates. This can be a simulated work environment set up by the school or a part-time temporary placement with a local employer. It is usually possible to find employers who will provide some training in exchange for free labor.

This internship or externship will provide students with a chance to experience directly the type of work they will be doing when they graduate. This can tie together work they have done in courses that might have seemed unrelated or irrelevant.

**Use several approaches**—It is difficult to predict just what change or which new program will have the most impact on student success. It is possible to spend so much time researching alternatives and looking for the "best" approach that nothing gets done. Experiment with several techniques at once. Several combined approaches will often be just what is needed.

**Put the most capable person in charge**—At most schools, there is no one person responsible for student success and retention. Often, "everyone is in charge" is the same as "no one is in charge." Find a person at your school who gets things done and put him in charge of improving the student retention rate. Find the most capable person and have him be the one responsible for decreasing student dropout.

Maybe that person is a teacher. Maybe he's an administrator. Maybe he is already working directly with students in a counseling center. Maybe that person is you. Whoever it is, give him a new job. Assign the job of improving student retention to one person. He can then get help from others in your school.

The person in charge of improving student retention can start by reviewing the ideas in this list and in other books written on student retention and establishing an action plan. The results of the plan can be monitored and measured, then revisions can be made to the plan. Through experimentation you will find what works at your school.

**Train tutors**—Student tutors and professional tutors alike need to be taught or reminded how to effectively encourage students to be academically successful. Set up a monthly meeting of all tutors and review basic teaching techniques and specific methods for being an effective tutor.

Faculty members from departments of education and outstanding teachers from any department of your school can be guest speakers at monthly tutor-training meetings. Also, frank and open discussions about the frustrations and successes of tutors can be valuable training.

**Provide a midpoint reward**—Halfway through their programs, provide each student with some type of recognition. This could be a certificate, a ceremony, a pin, a dinner, or any gesture that acknowledges their making it halfway.

There is a business school in the Northeast that teaches an airline and travel course. As a midpoint reward, it takes the students on a cruise to the Bahamas. The transportation costs are paid for by the school. Of course, overall tuition was raised to pay for the cost of the trip. In the long run, the school gains by a decrease in the dropout rate. This generous reward will not be possible at most schools. Stretch your imagination to find an appropriate way to congratulate students for completing half of their journey toward graduation.

**Adopt a student**—Look around and see who needs some special attention. Find a student whom you like and who you think needs extra encouragement. Adopt that student. Do what you can to ensure the success of that one person. This suggestion is sometimes criticized. People say that it is showing favoritism and partiality and seems to be suggesting that students should not all be treated the same. They are right—it is.

**Confess areas of ineffectiveness**—At least once a month, sit down with paper and pencil and take an honest inventory of your professional behavior. Look for what doesn't work in how you do your job. Consider the specific ways that you are ineffective.

Write them down. Take the time to closely examine what you do that doesn't work. Look for things you have done recently that have not promoted student success. Consider what you could change to improve the quality of your work.

This suggestion is not counter to positive thinking. It is great to have a positive self-image and to remind ourselves frequently of what we have done well. Nevertheless, it is also necessary to know what we have done that is not effective so that we can have an opportunity to change.

**Look through the eyes of the nontraditional student**—As demographic studies indicate, the average age of students is increasing. Students who return to school after several years often experience education differently. These students might have been homemakers, laborers, business operators, service men or women, world travelers, or hermits. They are likely to see things differently than a student fresh out of high school.

Take time to imagine how your school appears to the nontraditional student. Are the rules appropriate? Do lecture examples include older students? Is the atmosphere of student lounge facilities inviting and inclusive? Are activities designed to include everyone?

Explain the problems when recruiting. Students often approach school with unrealistic expectations. They might expect all the buildings to have tall columns and ivy. They might think their new instructors will be better than any they have ever had. They often imagine they will be attending Shangri-La U.

There are two distinct advantages to explaining problems when you recruit students. First, it brings expectations more in line with reality. Second, it raises the credibility of the person who is recruiting for the school.

Often people who recruit new students are seen strictly as salespeople. Their credibility might be questioned because it is their job to increase student enrollment. When they point out potential problems and the possible deficiencies of the school, they present a balanced report and possibly spare the student adjustment problems later on.

**Realize that some students are better off leaving**—Help them pack their bags. Not all students are meant to graduate. Their life goals might be best reached by leaving school. If this is the case, help them out. Really help them out.

Keep in mind that student retention improves when we promote student success. Sometimes, this means encouraging the student to stay in school even though it is very hard work, demanding personal sacrifice. Sometimes we might recommend leaving school.

**Use exit interviews**—Exit interviews can be conducted in person, by telephone, or through surveys. The key is to find out why students leave school. Many students do not officially drop out. They sort of fade away. At some point you know they are gone, and there was no time when they actually reported to a school official that they were leaving. In that case, the exit interview is more difficult to conduct, and it shouldn't be ignored. Exit interviews can be done over the phone with students who do not officially drop out. For those who cannot be reached by phone, a letter and a short questionnaire can provide the data.

The purpose of the exit interview is to find patterns in the many reasons why students drop out. A personal interview is the most effective way to gather this information. However, it will not work well if it is seen by the student as a way to talk him out of his decision to leave.

**Collect precise data and post it**—Many administrators do not know the exact data on their student retention rate. They know it is not what they want it to be, and they might even know approximately what it is. The strength of data comes from quantity and precision.

Each term, compute the retention rate of new and returning students. Compare this with precise figures from previous terms. Look for trends in programs, in types of students, and in the time of year.

Do a "by name" assessment. Knowing the number of students enrolled at the beginning of one term and the number enrolled at the beginning of the following term does not distinguish between predicted attrition and natural attrition. Predicted attrition involves students who have expressed their intention to leave after one term and might not indicate any problems that can be corrected. Raw numbers from one term to the next do not account for late arrivals who enroll after the term begins. Also, these numbers do not compare the retention rates of students who have taken a Student Success course with those who have not. Knowing the precise attributes of students who have been retained and those who have not can suggest specific strategies to improve retention.

Make this data available to those people who have the most influence on student success. They can look for more effective ways to promote student success and can celebrate improvements in retention rates.

Forget about improving retention. Concentrate on improving student success. Dropout rates will consequently decrease.

**Set up a prepayment program**—Allow students to make advance payments on the anticipated difference between their financial aid award and the cost of their education. If for some reason the student did not start classes, this prepayment would be refunded with interest accrued.

The advantage of this system goes beyond encouraging wise budgeting. A prepayment is a form of commitment. It demonstrates in one more way a student's determination to start or to continue his education.

Use flextime for student problem solving. It is difficult for some students to complete their financial aid forms, pay their bills, register for their classes, pick up their test papers, or meet with their instructors between 8 a.m. and 5 p.m. It might serve students' needs if some offices were open for extended weekday hours and on Saturday mornings.

**Recruit graduates**—Rather than recruiting freshmen who might drop out, admissions personnel can recruit students who are likely to graduate. Entrance examinations can be used to help students decide if they have a reasonable chance of being successful in your school.

Academically underprepared students and students with career interests not served by your school are unlikely to become graduates. Consider discouraging their enrollment.

**Establish developmental programs**—For those students who are academically underprepared, provide a way for them to strengthen their skills. It is possible to significantly improve basic reading, writing, and mathematics skills in a short time. Set up classes or individual learning experiences in which students can prepare themselves academically.

Basic math and English courses are available as elective courses, required courses, or independent, self-paced study programs. These are often competency based, so students' progress can be monitored and a level of performance required before they are allowed to register for the next term. Small classes with specially trained instructors generally have excellent results in increasing basic skills. Students are then prepared to be successful.

**Intervene**—This notion is foreign to many educators who grew up with the philosophy to "live and let live." It seems somehow old-fashioned and even inappropriate to get involved in another person's life. Consider doing it anyway.

When students begin their post-secondary education, they do it out of choice. They select a school on the basis of many factors, including where they think they can be successful. In a real sense, they buy that chance for success with their tuition dollars. They are entering into a contract that says, "If I do this . . . , I will get this. . . ." They expect to graduate and to receive all of the benefits associated with graduating. And they expect to do what is required to get to graduation. Often we don't tell them what is required. We don't want to meddle, to intrude, to interfere.

To intervene is appropriate when you have been given permission. By their choice to pursue graduating from your school, students have given that permission. They have, in a sense, said, "Tell me periodically how I am doing in my quest for graduation." It therefore seems appropriate to report what you see.

This reporting might even include the following approaches. In a telephone call to the home of a student, you might say, "I am concerned about your attendance. Your absence today was the fourth this term." After a class, you might tell the student, "I wonder if you're having a difficult time sticking with what is happening in class. It looks like your attention is seldom on the lecture or the class discussion." In a letter, you might write, "Please call me or see me after class and make an appointment to discuss your progress. I want you to be successful."

**Set up an emergency loan fund**—"For the want of a nail the war was lost." Sometimes a few dollars are all that is needed to survive a financial crisis. A twenty-dollar loan might solve the current emergency and prevent a more drastic solution, such as dropping out to get a job.

In times of financial stress, it is difficult to keep long-term goals firmly in mind. Priorities seem to rearrange themselves, and getting a few dollars becomes all important. An emergency loan fund can be a temporary solution to short-term financial problems.

This emergency loan would have low interest, a modest limit ($30 to $80), and a short term (two to four months). The loan could be processed quickly and the money disbursed within minutes of application. At some schools, this type of loan has been financed by student contributions and fundraisers.

**Challenge students**—Boredom can be tolerated if it is not pervasive. Students will generally put up with a lot of tedium if they have one thing that is challenging. Provide some opportunity for stretching. Academic adventure can be provided by extraordinary class projects, unusual assignments, outside readings that allow for creativity, or substitute classes. Even one independent study class or project within a class can be an avenue for academic challenge.

**Invert the curriculum**—The traditional college curriculum postpones "major" courses until the second or third year of study. A freshman excited about psychology is likely to get his first "real" course only after several semesters of general education. Inverting the curriculum would allow the student to begin his study of psychology first thing.

This same approach can be applied in each class. Material that students consider the "real thing" can be presented up front. Foundations do need to be laid, and this can be done along with the material that students consider to be the "meat" of the course. In a computer course, students can be taught to write a computer program on the first day. In an accounting course, a simple financial statement for a well-known business can be reviewed immediately. In a chemistry course, an experiment can be performed by each student during the first week.

**Institute a retention bonus**—Consider paying staff and faculty a year-end bonus based on a decrease in the student dropout rate. Profit in proprietary schools is almost a direct function of student retention rates. Revenue in private schools is directly affected by student retention. Even many public institutions are immediately affected by student dropouts. A retention bonus assumes that employees of the school have a direct effect on student retention and that people are motivated by money.

A bonus to all employees need not be evenly distributed. Those people who have the most direct student contact could be eligible for a larger bonus. All bonuses would be dependent on the school's meeting a predetermined improvement in the retention rate, and further improvements might even raise the amount of the bonus. For example, if the retention rate of first-term students improved by at least 5 percent of the average retention rate of the previous three years, then each instructor teaching first-term students would receive a $400 bonus, and all other teachers and employees would receive $200.

(CAUTION: As with all suggestions, this one abounds with potential—potential benefits and potential trouble. Standards have to be maintained. Fairness is always questioned. Educators do not like to be seen as mercenary. And money is an excellent motivator that often gets people to discover new and effective ways to promote student success.)

**Examine attitudes at financial aid and business offices**—Unknowingly, people who work with students and money can fall into a pattern of being patronizing and condescending. Awareness is the key to change.

**Develop in-service for faculty to set the stage for faculty development**—This can include daylong workshops with outside presenters or monthly meetings in which discussion centers on how classes can be conducted more effectively. The material presented does not have to be new and innovative to be effective. Often we just need to be reminded to continue to use that which we know works.

A useful format for faculty development is one in which teachers are encouraged to brainstorm suggestions for improving classroom instruction, student services, and administrative operations and policies. These brainstorms, occurring at the beginning of each meeting, can get energy flowing and set the stage for useful discussion. Remember that the purpose of the brainstorm is quantity, not quality, and outrageous ideas often lead to the discovery of the best suggestions.

Brainstormed lists can be typed and distributed for future discussion and evaluation. Evaluation of brainstorms is most effective when done with selection as a goal rather than deletion. That is, time can be spent selecting items to be expanded or implemented, rather than spending time deleting those items that are considered ridiculous or unworkable.

**Use student representatives on committees**—It is generally easier to accept policies and decisions that we have a hand in making. Students generally take committee assignments very seriously. An alternative to this might be to set up a president's advisory board composed of students.

**Examine housing conditions**—Look at where students are living. This might include campus housing or local apartment complexes. If housing conditions are not conducive to success, discuss with students the impact of living environments on success. Search for alternatives and help them improve their housing conditions.

**Get a commitment to return after breaks**—Look for ways to get students to indicate their intention to return to school after each break. Over vacations and between terms are likely times for students to decide to drop out of school. You can get some idea that this might occur if students are reluctant to share their plans about the future.

Ways to get some type of commitment include preregistration, course project preliminary plans (have students submit an outline of what their class projects will involve), prepayment of tuition or fees, and surveys. Informally, this commitment can be requested verbally—"Is everything set for you for next term?"

**Make helpers highly visible**—Students who need assistance might not be aggressive in looking for help. Advisors, counselors, tutors, financial aid officers, and other student services personnel can be made visible by office location, bulletin board advertisements, brochures, and frequent class announcements promoting student services.

**Set up a summer (prestart) orientation program**—Sometime before classes actually start, reach every student on campus. Personal contact with school personnel and the facilities will increase the chances that the student starts class and is successful.

**Provide day care**—As the number of older students starting school increases, the needs of the student body change. Finding competent and trusted care for children is an activity that occupies hours of many students' lives. It is possible to provide day care without actually operating a center.

Locate a day care center close to school and set up a referral program. Some centers will provide discounts for members of certain groups, such as students attending your school.

**Individualize instruction**—It might not be practical to allow students to progress at their own rate in every class they take. It is desirable to allow self-directed and self-paced instruction in at least some part of at least one class every term. Most students want the independence of choosing their own direction.

Individualized instruction provides a way for students to feel some autonomy and to take responsibility for some aspect of their education. It gives the student who does not function well in a rigid system a chance to set his own pace. Advanced students can have the experience of racing forward, and underachieving students can move at a pace that allows them to master the material.

**Review policies and rules**—Students report that meaningless rules and regulations are one of their greatest frustrations and a frequent reason that they drop out of school. It might not be possible to change all of the rules that students find objectionable, yet it is possible to modify policies and rules that no longer make sense.

We are habitual animals, and our institutions model our rigidity. There might be dozens of rules and regulations at your school that could be changed with no harm done to the purposes and goals of your institution. A policy that made perfect sense when it was developed fifty years ago might now need to be changed.

Ask students what doesn't make sense and then see what you can change. When you are asking for student opinion, make it clear that you cannot follow all of their suggestions. Stress that you will do all you can to accommodate their needs.

98

**Set up an advocacy program**—Consider assigning one advocate or advisor to every group of 10 to 15 students. These advocates can be faculty members, staff, or administrators. Their purpose would be to meet with the group of students and identify ways in which they could help the students achieve their goals.

These group meetings would begin immediately after the start of school and would be scheduled at least once a month during the first term and less frequently thereafter. During the meetings, students would get a chance to meet several other students, talk about goals, make suggestions, discuss frustrations and accomplishments, ask questions, and receive specific tips on adjusting to a new environment.

Encourage regular attendance at the meetings and follow up on each student who does not attend. Specific problems and suggestions can be communicated by the advocate to the appropriate school personnel.

**Establish extracurricular activities**—Even the smallest school can have a program of extracurricular activities. Having a football team or a symphony orchestra is not the only way to get students involved with each other outside of the classroom. A bowling club or barbershop quartet can accomplish the same thing. Set up some way for students to become involved with the school and with other students outside of academics.

**Write or update an advisory handbook**—The people at your school who advise students often learn by legend. They pass on to students what has been passed on to them. What they advise might be wrong, even though a lot of people believe it. Constructing or revising a handbook might lead to clarification of policies and rules that have become mysteries.

**Select advisors carefully**—Not all teachers are suited to advise students. A person might interact very well with a group of students and not interact well in one-on-one situations. Selection is most effective when it starts with self-selection. People often know when they wouldn't do an effective job. And others will say that they just don't want to. It is unlikely that you would want people who don't like that type of work to be advising.

**Solicit schoolwide support**—Ask everyone to be involved in the job of promoting student success. It is possible to just clean the classrooms, and it is possible to clean the classrooms with the idea of promoting student success. The job is done differently in subtle and significant ways.

When we do our work with the purpose of helping students, we usually find ways that we can do the job more effectively. (Working efficiently is doing a job right; working effectively is doing the right job right.) Every teacher, administrator, and staff member can have an impact on student success every day.

**Schedule a Faculty and Staff Appreciation Day**—Form a committee composed of administrators, faculty, staff, and students to plan a special day to honor the faculty and staff. Fun and food can be combined with sincere expressions of gratitude. Perhaps the student government would like to be responsible for this event.

**Schedule a Student Appreciation Day**—Form a committee to plan a special day to honor students. Improved morale contributes to improved retention rates. Administrators, faculty, and staff can be creative and brainstorm a long list of ways to demonstrate their appreciation of students.

**Ask others to get involved**—Set up a task force on student success that cuts across all areas of the college. Post the purpose of "serve students" in prominent places as a reminder for all to see. Send letters internally reporting on what is being done specifically to promote student success and asking for ideas. Get everyone involved.

**Establish a required, ongoing orientation program**—College Survival is available to help schools implement continuing orientation classes. This type of course would meet at least once a week for a minimum of 30 contact hours and would be required of all full-time, nontransfer students as a for-credit course. The course covers study skills and life skills appropriate for being successful in school, and it encourages the use of school and community resources.

Assume the validity of the Power Process "I create it all." Consider for a moment the ridiculous notion that you are responsible for every student who drops out of school. Then look for ways that you create those dropouts. By using this idea, you might discover strategies for promoting student success that you never would have otherwise considered.

**Support warmth, friendliness, and caring**—An environment of love is apparent, even though it cannot easily be defined. People can feel when they are in a place that is friendly, warm, and caring. The way to effect this change is simple and requires lots of energy. Commit to the change and talk it up. In every interaction and in every conversation, each of us can communicate our warmth, friendliness, and caring. It soon becomes contagious.

## The role of faculty in retaining students on campus

Stressing the benefits of staying in school is an essential part of eliciting support for your course. Depending on course content, following are some of the benefits students can expect:

- Difficult tasks, assignments, and papers take less time.
- Learning obstacles disappear.
- Employability is enhanced.
- Investment in education is more likely to pay off.
- School is more enjoyable.
- Grades improve.
- Studying is more productive.
- Academic, career, and life goals are in focus.
- Anxiety level is reduced.
- More hours are available for fun, work, study, or sleep.
- Notes are legible and useful.
- Inquiry skills improve.
- Tests are approached more confidently and skillfully.
- Stressful situations are easier to handle.
- Choice of school or major is clarified.
- Policies and rules that govern the institution are understood.
- Communication skills improve.
- Technology is utilized more effectively.
- Support groups are established.
- Self-confidence increases.
- Involvement in the educational community increases.
- Procrastination diminishes.

100

- Relationships improve with spouses, teachers, roommates, friends, parents, children, and so on.
- Money is managed better.
- Campus and community resources become more familiar.
- Endorsement by the faculty is critical to the foundation of your Student Success course.

Faculty support can include the following steps:
- Promote the academic credibility of your course, recognize its creditworthiness, and take appropriate action, if necessary, in the faculty senate or curriculum committee in order to get the course approved.
- Provide feedback to Student Success course instructors about student needs and/or deficiencies. Later, faculty can provide information about how your course is influencing student behavior.
- Speak positively about your course to students, parents, administrators, and fellow faculty members.
- Take part in a retention task force or orientation committee.
- Be directly involved through teaching, team teaching, or facilitating one or more sections.
- Participate in your course as a guest speaker.
- Reinforce concepts and methods introduced in the Student Success course and incorporate them into individual disciplines.
- Refer students to your course (if the course isn't mandatory).

Here are some course benefits that might be of interest to the faculty:
- Teaching is more productive and enjoyable. Students are awake, active, responsible for their learning, and task oriented. Students learn to teach themselves.
- Students who acquire lifelong learning skills have a greater appreciation for education and for the teachers who provide an opportunity for learning.
- Improved retention results in greater revenue and high student numbers. These in turn can increase demand for faculty, create support to improve facilities, and, in terms of budget cuts, enhance the security of teaching positions.
- College survival courses provide an unusual opportunity to interact with students on a personal level.
- More upper-division classes are available to teach due to the increased number of upper class students.
- Faculty members who teach this type of course enjoy additional benefits. Being a part of the exciting discoveries students make and observing changes in student attitudes can renew one's sense of what is possible in education.

## The role of administrators in retaining students on campus

Administrators provide key elements in support of Student Success courses. Ask them to contribute to the success of the course in such ways as the following:
- Recognizing the potential of your course and including it as an essential part of the institutional retention plan
- Promoting the activity of a retention task force or committee. This can include scheduling and announcing meetings, requesting members to participate actively and perform specific tasks, and setting timelines.

- Ensuring that your course carries academic credit if that is within administrative control. College survival courses can be a viable part of a core curriculum. In many instances, they fulfill general education requirements.
- Making your course mandatory for all new students, if appropriate
- Listing your course in the catalog and enrollment documents as a legitimate part of the curriculum
- Scheduling your course in attractive time slots
- Taking responsibility for the details of registration. It is common for a newly required Student Success course to falter at registration if some workers are unaware that scheduling each student into the course is mandatory.
- Ensuring that rooms and equipment are available and adequate
- Participating as guest speakers
- Teaching or facilitating one or more sections. Although this might go beyond the typical show of support, it would be a substantial demonstration of the administration's belief in the importance of your course. Presidents, vice presidents, and deans often make excellent teachers of a Student Success course. Participating in this way can also enhance their relationships with students.
- Publicly voicing their support of your course to students, faculty, and other administrators
- Selecting instructors who care about student success. Ideally, teachers will give students an opportunity to experiment with new methods and techniques rather than merely lecturing about them.

When asking for these and other measures of support from administrators, emphasize course benefits that will affect them specifically, such as the following:

- Enhanced student performance as measured by grade point averages, number of courses completed per term per student, and persistence to graduation.
- Stronger financial position of the department and institution due to a higher number of paying customers. Most schools spend heavily on recruiting and matriculating new students. When these students leave before graduating, they must be replaced, again at high cost. Cutting attrition simultaneously cuts revenue losses.
- More satisfied clients, making it easier to recruit new students. Successful students have positive things to say about your school in their circle of influence. When they graduate and are employed, they can act as models and recruiters for your institution.
- Improved student feedback. A Student Success course can provide a new channel for communication between students and the administrators.
- More satisfied faculty. Teaching students who take responsibility for their learning can decrease faculty frustration and complaints. Students bring new learning skills to their other classes and might incidentally help their instructors become more effective. Your course will stimulate new conversations among faculty about teaching and learning.

The following are additional benefits:

- Enhanced faculty awareness about retention
- Reduced need for crisis counseling. Your course can head off little problems before they turn into exit interviews.
- High visibility and more effective use of career counselors, tutors, substance abuse programs, and other campus resources
- A new marketing tool for recruiting. The existence of a Student Success course is evidence of your institution's commitment to the success of its students. It can also be used as a way to ease a prospective student's anxiety about his academic skills and ability to cope with college pressures. Inform your admissions staff of the benefits of your

Student Success course. Consider providing a copy of your course textbook to each admissions representative. Knowing the benefits and having a copy of the textbook to show to students can make her job easier.

## Creating a pre- and post-course assessment on your campus

*This section was contributed to by Laura Goppold, Discipline Chair, Academic Related Courses and Director, Special Projects at Central Piedmont Community College*

Since it's inception at Central Piedmont Community College (CPCC) in 1995, Academic Related classes have served an average of 600 students each year in the College Study Skills course, ACA 118. This course is a two credit hour course that meets for 150 minutes each week and is a general elective. Students at CPCC are *not* required to take this course. As you may be experiencing on your campus, ever-tightening budgets create priorities for spending wherein efficacy and accountability become crucial indicators for funding.

More directly, as a College Study Skills instructor for nearly eight years at Central Piedmont Community College, I often wondered how much my students really "got" out of my class. It seemed that no matter where I focused my energy for the class– textbook, active learning techniques, learning styles, critical thinking, or peer collaboration—I was concerned about whether the learning and the skills were sustained long enough to help them succeed in classes the following semester. Anecdotal information in the form of an occasional positive reference about the course by instructors outside of the discipline, and students' grades were not adequate indicators of student success. I talked to other instructors within the College Success courses at CPCC and they expressed the same concern.

Looking at grades and grading systems, we realized that there is no uniform way to measure the learning across the Student Success sections within our entire college system. This is true for all courses, not just study skills courses. While many assignments are uniform, course delivery, requirements, and grading systems are, in keeping with CPCC's emphasis on academic freedom, unique to individual instructors. Active learning (and teaching) strategies, journaling, group interaction, instructor interviews, service learning, learning communities, and visitation to campus resources were the work of the course, but they were not providing the outcome assessments we needed.

**What did we want to know?** Learning cannot be measured adequately by any single assessment. At CPCC, we knew that a test could only show us patterns of success and failure. These patterns, however, could give us some clues about the teaching and the learning occurring at our school.

**What did we do?** Creating a pre-test post-test for *Becoming a Master Student* (Tenth Edition) allowed us to determine what information students retained throughout the course. We began assessing our students in the Fall of 2002 and over the next five semesters. We administered a pre- and post- course assessment of 56 questions related to the first seven chapters of the textbook.

The pre-test was administered within the first two weeks of each semester to determine what, if anything, students already knew. Because of the varying backgrounds students have coming into college, we expected that our students came to CPCC with varying levels of knowledge and skill in goal setting, time management, memory, note-taking, reading, test-taking strategies, and critical thinking.

The post-test was administered after the first seven chapters had been covered in class. The questions on the post-test were the same questions that appeared on the pre-test. Measuring the differences from pre to post-test administration allowed us to measure what information was learned, and what was retained.

The information that we gleaned from this process has helped us to restructure our course priorities based on students' needs and visible trends. At CPCC, a group of study skills instructors (some who teach in other areas of the college) analyzed the data to determine ways to address less successful areas and ways to capitalize and enhance our talents in the successful areas. This information and the process itself could then be shared with other instructors, departments, and divisions.

This process helps our students as teachers develop new strategies to approach the skills from various learning styles and modalities.

If you are interested in administering a pre- and post- course assessment to your students, to measure content retention, materials are available on the HM ClassPrep CD with a revised assessment that is comparable to the content in the Eleventh Edition of *Becoming a Master Student*. Tips on how to administer the test, measure the results, and share them with Houghton Mifflin Company (such that they could then be shared with other faculty) are available on the CD.

## Creating evaluations of your course

**Course Rationale** The methods you use and the questions you ask to measure outcomes are determined by the purpose of your evaluation. Evaluating course effectiveness helps you discover specific ways to improve the course and provides a rationale for its continuation and expansion.

Evaluations can highlight improvements that will help your course meet its objectives. Teacher effectiveness, selection of content, skills application, and methods of instruction can all be evaluated and improved. Ongoing evaluations can help you make continual adjustments, fine-tune the content, and improve your teaching strategies. Following are some areas you might want to investigate to help you refine the purpose of your course and improve it.

### Students
- Does the course meet students' needs?
- Do students take responsibility for their own education?
- Are students able to transfer skills to other classes?
- Are students learning to be active, independent thinkers?
- Do students gain greater confidence in their learning ability?
- Is the course interactive?
- Are students given a voice in what is presented in class?

### Instructors
- Do instructors vary their methods to teach to all learning styles?
- Do instructors assess which teaching methods worked well and which didn't?
- Do instructors communicate effectively?
- Are instructors ambitious about the course?
- Do instructors invite and facilitate student participation?
- Are instructors following the seven-part course structure?
- Do students participate actively in conversations and sharing?
- Are instructors limiting their lecture time?
- Are students asked to make commitments?

104

- Are students being held accountable to their commitments?
- Do instructors demonstrate how students can transfer skills?
- Are students encouraged to give honest feedback?

**Content**
- How could the course be changed to make it more effective?
- Which topics were well received by students and which were not?
- Which guest speakers elicited positive responses from students?
- Are appropriate guest speakers invited to the class?
- Is the faculty being consulted about what to include in the course?
- Is the course flexible enough to respond to student needs?
- Can your upper class students or alumni provide insight into course improvements?

**Course Continuation and Expansion** Administrators are more willing to continue a course and even expand it when the course meets outlined objectives. Evaluations help administrators make choices. Following are some areas to consider:

- Is adequate credit given for the course?
- Are there sufficient contact hours to achieve course objectives?
- What impact does the course have on the institution's financial position?
- Should additional class sections be offered?
- Will requiring the class of all students increase retention?
- How can the effectiveness of the course be demonstrated?
- Are qualified instructors recruited to teach the course?
- Are the strategies taught being reinforced in other classes?
- Are instructors of other courses noticing behavioral changes in students?
- Are there objections to the course? If so, what are they?
- How can the course benefit recruitment?
- Does the course influence the student counseling load?
- Does the course influence the use of career counselors?
- Does the course influence the use of tutors and other resources?
- Does the course influence the use of the school library?
- What evidence provides justification for a required course?
- What evidence provides justification for an expanded course?
- Is the course scheduled at reasonable time periods?
- What information would be useful for the retention task force or committee?

**Outcomes** Student Success courses encourage behavioral changes in areas related to being a successful student. Outcomes are results that can be measured. Once you gather the data, there are several ways to analyze and interpret it. You can use matched pair correlations, select students randomly to be in the course, or design longitudinal, split group, or control group studies to compare students who take the class with those who don't. Following are questions to ask when determining outcomes.

**What Are Retention Rates Over Time?**
- What are first-term retention rates?
- What are first-, second-, and third-year retention rates?
- What percentage of students graduate or complete their programs?

- How do the retention rates of students who took the course differ from the retention rates of those who didn't?
- How do the graduation rates of students who took the course differ from the graduation rates of those who didn't?
- If the course is now required, how do current retention rates compare with retention rates before it was required?

## What Effect Does the Course Have on Grade Point Averages?
- How does the GPA of students who took the course differ from the GPA of those who didn't?
- Do students who take the course improve and maintain their GPAs better than those who don't take the course?

## What Is the Course's Impact on the Number of Credits Completed per Term?
- Do students who take the course complete more credits than those who don't?
- Do students who take the course complete a larger percentage of credits attempted than those who don't?

## What Is the Course's Impact on Students' Intentions to Stay in School?
- Do students who take the course intend to stay in school longer than those who don't?

## How Does the Course Affect Student Participation in School?
- Do students who take the course participate more in school activities (sports, plays, cultural events, social programs, etc.)?
- Do students who take the course participate more in student organizations (government, social and academic clubs, etc.)?
- Do students who take the course take on more leadership roles?

## How Does the Course Affect Student Use of School Resources?
- Are students who take the course better informed about school resources?
- Do students who take the course make more appointments with faculty and counselors?
- Do students who take the course visit the library more frequently?
- Do students who take the course use tutors more often?

**Methods** There are several methods of determining the effectiveness of the Student Success course. The ultimate measures of course effectiveness are improved student performance and increased retention rates. Following are some ideas about how to evaluate your course.

## Frequent Content and Process Evaluations
- Ask students to evaluate both the content and process.
- Request feedback from students on regular class quizzes.
- Note improvement in quiz scores as the term progresses.
- Note improvement in test scores in all other courses.
- Ask other instructors to attend and evaluate your course.
- Ask for feedback from other instructors about students' performance.
- Ask administrators to attend and evaluate your course.
- Ask students for feedback during conversations and sharing.
- Videotape students in class, observe their reactions, and evaluate the effectiveness of classroom activities.

- Ask students to interview other students and get recommendations.

**Evaluations of the Instructor**
- Evaluate yourself after each class period.
- Videotape yourself and critique your style and communication.
- Videotape yourself and ask others to critique your presentation.
- Ask other instructors to attend and evaluate your teaching.

**Final Evaluations**
- Conduct a thorough and anonymous final evaluation.
- Do an in-depth self-evaluation at the end of the term.
- Survey the faculty about student attitudes and performance.
- Compare student pre- and post-course scores on assessment instruments.
- Compare internal and external locus of control scores.
- Interview students on videotape.
- Compare students' perceptions of their progress on the Discovery Wheel from the beginning to the end of the term.
- Interview individual students to discover what they gained and what changes they recommend.

**Follow-Up Evaluations**
- Do a follow-up evaluation a few months after the course has ended.
- Form a faculty course evaluation committee.
- Form a student course evaluation committee.
- Form a combined student and faculty course evaluation committee.

Start now: Evaluate today's class

Here is an example of a critical incident classroom questionnaire. (Acknowledgment to Stephen D. Brookfield, *Becoming a Critically Reflective Teacher*.)

Ask your students to take about five minutes to respond to each of the following questions about today's class. They do not need to put their name on the form—their responses should be anonymous. When they have finished writing, have them put the form on a table by the door. At the start of the next class, begin by sharing the responses with the group. Remember to thank your students for taking the time to do this. These responses will help you make your class more responsive to their concerns.

1.   At what moment today did you feel most engaged with what was happening?

2.   At what moment in class did you feel most distanced from what was happening?

3.   What actions by the teacher and/or students did you find most affirming and helpful?

4.   What actions by the teacher and/or students did you find most puzzling or confusing?

5.   What about the class this week surprised you the most? What will you use?